The Silent Revolution of Generation X

by Simone Sturm

To all GenXers in the World

CONTENTS

1. FOREWORD

The first rule of Gen X is... you do not talk about Gen X!

This motto from the movie "Fight Club" in 1999 with Edward Norton and Brad Pitt sums it all up pretty well: Nobody talks about this demographic cohort. Many GenXers themselves don't even know which generation they belong to. But why is that?

Most of the GenXers I have interviewed for my research, simply don't care. We feel like as if we didn't belong to a group. Most are independent and don't like to be categorized. Probably because we don't feel the necessity for that. Very different from other generations who love to talk about themselves: Baby Boomers, Millennials and Generation Z for example. All the cool things that they have done, achieved and invented. We all know the stories of Steve Jobs, Bill Gates, Mark Zuckerberg and Greta Thunberg.

But GenXers? For some reason that's not the case and there is very little information about this cohort on the internet and social media at all. If you try to google "Generation X" you will find the 1970s English punk rock band by Billy Idol and few other articles. And that's about it. Not much about this demographic group. I didn't care much either until lately I had stumbled upon some videos and articles about Generation X written by Baby Boomers or Millennials. Most of the concepts were simply wrong. They had no idea. That's when I decided that if *anybody* should write about Generation X, it should be one of us.

I did my research for a year, reading articles, comment sections, books and statistics. I've interviewed people from many different backgrounds and countries. Watched movies and YouTube videos I reckoned relevant to this topic. Patiently I've collected all the small pieces of the puzzle. They matched together perfectly. And I finally saw the big picture. We've been neglected, overlooked and forgotten about for way to long. It's time to step out of the shadow. I proudly present to you *my* Generation:

Generation X.

Generation what?

What if I told you that we have brought to you YouTube and Google, Wikipedia and Whats App? Do you even know who are the people behind these inventions? No idea? All GenXers. Millions of people use these services every day, we couldn't imagine our modern lives without them. But hardly anybody knows the names of the founders. As if their inventions had been around forever. But they have not. Somebody has actually invented them and *given* them to the world. And they are for *free*.

Doesn't that make you wonder about Gen X? Let me take you back with me in time and discover the origins of this forgotten generation.

2. DISCLAIMER

I always thought that my memories were only based on personal experiences. Maybe I had misinterpreted the things that I had witnessed as a child, or my fantasy had deformed my remembrance. I was sure to be alone because everybody on TV, socials and the internet seemed to have a completely different perception of life.

But then I found out, that there were many people in different places who had experienced the *exact same* things. Simply nobody had ever talked about it. So I researched historical events, statistics and newspapers of that time. I was blown away. My feelings and memories were real, it wasn't my imagination, they were based on real facts.

We have just been denied and overlooked the whole time. Everybody has a different story, background and opinion, that's perfectly fine. I just wrote down what I felt and drew my own conclusions, you are free to disagree.

I didn't mean to offend anybody, neither younger or elder generations. I hope that we can all accept and start learning from each other one day. Each generation has its strengths and its weaknesses. If we started working together instead of blaming each other we could create a better future for all.

3. THE FORGOTTEN MIDDLE-CHILD

Lately you might have followed the heated discussion between the "Baby Boomers" and the "Millennials" on social media, in TV and talk shows.

The 55-75 year-old against young adults in their late 20s and 30s. There are shows, memes and even games entitled "Boomers vs Millennials", like the one aired on the talk show "Ellen" and as a parody on SNL. They confront the contestants and make fun of some Millennials who don't know how to read an analog clock or Baby Boomers who don't know what 'Earbuds' are.

We can watch endless discussions about the Baby Boomers accusing the Millennials for their attitude and the Millennials blaming the Baby Boomers of destroying the world. It goes on and on. Maybe you have followed some of this dispute with curiosity and amusement like me, until an inevitably question arose:

What group do I belong to? Is it the elder generation against the young? What does that have to do with me? What are they talking about? And most of all: why is everybody yelling all the time and nobody ever let's the other finish a sentence? Maybe you don't really recognize yourself in neither one nor the other. You are definitely not a 60-something all self-entitled and self-indulgent but neither a 30-year-old Millennial, even if we completely agree with the arguments against the Baby Boomers. But there's something we don't understand about their attitude either, like showing little patience and becoming so easily offended and upset.

So what are we? We feel like we don't belong to neither one. Maybe we *are* different. Maybe we *don't* fit in. We've *never* fit in. There's a good reason why we feel like that. We simply *don't*. We were born between two very self-centered, demanding and noisy cohorts and that's why we have forgotten even ourselves that we actually are part of a generation of its *own*.

They call it "the *Generation X*"

Where the 'X' stands for the unknown, the undefined. We've never even gotten a a real name. Generations have been named and classified in different books and statistics in the 20century but there is no absolute reference because the matter is quite arbitrary and the boundaries fuzzy.

Let's have a look at the main guidelines:

The two theorists Neil Howe and William Strauss created the following list of generation names in their US 1991 book entitled "Generations":

1924 and earlier "Greatest Generation"

1925-1942 "Silent Generation"

1946-1964 "Baby Boomers"

1965-1979 "Generation X"

(other sources reach from 1963 until 1983)

1980-2000 "Millennials" or "Gen Y"

2000-2015 "Gen Z" or the "i-Generation"

2015- today "Generation Alpha"

So Generation X includes roughly people born between the mid 60s and early 80s. There is also a micro-generation of Cuspers which ranges from the late 1970s to the mid 80s. That demographic cohort is called by the media "the Xennials", with characteristics from both generations, Gen X and Millennials.

I don't want to list all the statistics here, you can easily find them on the internet. It's already interesting that in most cases generations cover a 20-year span (like Baby Boomers and Millennials) while Generation X is reduced to 14-15 years in most statistics.

Why did we get 5 years less than others? I also wonder after The "Greatest Generation", the "Silent Generation" and "Baby Boomers" what could possibly go wrong to call the next Generation just "Gen X"? Lack of ideas? Seems as if the previous generations didn't consider us as being important at all. They have been calling us 'slackers' for all our lives and says a lot about what they think about us.

Canadian author Douglas Coupland, born in 1961, called us the "Generation X" in his book "Generation X, tales for an accelerated culture" which was published in 1991. He uses "X" for the uncatalogued, the variable in mathematical equations and also the desire of not to be defined." It wasn't meant to be the Roman letter X (10), because in the ranking we saw earlier Neil Howe and William Strauss wanted to call us the "13th generation" (after the independence) but that name never really caught on. So that doesn't explain the X either.

In the final chapter of the funny sociological book "Class" by Paul Fussel in 1983, the "X" is a

"category of people who wanted to hop off the merry-go-round of status, money and social climbing that so often frames modern existence".

That defines our cohort better. We always wanted to be different and not comply with the rules of modern life.

I find also the definition of "the X Files" as in the homonymous series from 1993 until 2018 to be on point.

"Everything that cannot be filed in any other folder is collected here".

We started out as a Generation without a real name and hardly any consideration whatsoever. And that hasn't changed much until today. Otherwise how do you explain that there are " Boomers vs Millennials" all over the media and nobody ever even mentions Gen X?

Also the author and entrepreneur Robert Kiyosaki, who writes books about financial education, always talks about *"the lucky Baby Boomers"* and *"the financially screwed Millennials"*.

No GenXers mentioned at any time.

As if we didn't even *exist*..

4. GENERATIONS

Quick introduction to the different cohorts we are talking about:

Members of The **Silent Generation**, born between 1925 and 1942 have witnessed World War II, the great depression and seriously hard times. They know well about sacrifice and commitment, most of them have built houses with their own hands, have lived through poverty and carry inside the deep fear of loosing it all. Mostly very frugal they have strong work ethics, are dedicated to their families, work, respectful of authorities and mostly very traditional in their mindset.

The **Baby Boomers** 1943 -1964 are children of the post war. The name derives from the pike of babies born after WWII. The economic boom of the 50s and 60s allowed the Boomers to grow up in an optimistic environment. With a medium education they could find jobs quite easily at a very young age, which they would keep for a lifetime. Prices and taxes were low and they were the only ones to live the capitalism where the middle class could afford to have only one parent working and the other staying at home. Yet afford a house, a car, a TV and a decent lifestyle. This is the only generation that has seen mayor benefits from their employer, in some countries even a 35 hour work week while keeping full wages and some retired in their early 50s. Many kept on working as external consultant and received double wages.

They grew up in the 1950s and 1960s when the world was growing, witnessed the first man on the moon, there was optimism and faith in the power of people, the future and economic expansion.

In the 1970s and 1980s, when Boomers were in theirs 20s and 30s, countless new music styles were born, they've had Woodstock, the 68s, experimented drugs, started a political rebellion and the hippie movement.

With the invention of birth control women could make their own family plans and the sexual revolution had just started. Boomers gained a strong identity, very flashy, loud and demanding. There were less rules, people would drive without safety belts, there were no safety cameras anywhere and people would get away with almost anything.

With them growing up society had shifted from being a *"culture of the child"* in the 50s towards a *"culture of the adult"* in the 1970s. This phenomenon has been described in the book "Abort Retry Ignore Fail" 1993 by Strauss and Howe.

So they have *always* been in the center of attention, growing up *and* as adults. Parental self-actualization was just as important as civil rights, adult life in general and entertainment. The world of business was an empty canvas to paint, anybody could invent, create and make their own fortune. Brands were born, music and fashion-labels founded and there was no end to creativity. With a strong self-esteem they had all the power to change things in society. They fought for civil rights for women, same sex couples, against racism and saw some change happening. They always stood up and said everything they wanted

. Their parents told them to "get the world, it's yours to take". And that's what they did. Too bad they did this literally. They went out and took it. All of it. All the resources, all the environment, all the money.

Probably they are the last generation to receive a pension that you can live on. In the late 1960s and 1970s the global destruction of the environment was already at a dramatic point. Plastic, oil, cars, smog and water pollution. When money was tight the government just decided to print more.

In 1971 the Nixon administration converted the dollar from *money* into a *currency*, so they could freely print all the dollars they wanted to. Creating more and more debts, to leave to the generations to come.

And that's when the **GenXers** were born. In the late 1960s and 1970s, society had just changed from a child-centered to an adult-centered world where the rights and interests of adults were more important than child care.

When we were kids, the world was a tumultuous place. Flashy and loud clothing, revolutionary music, people smoking everywhere and everybody had a strong attitude towards everything. Children were not the center of the universe and pedagogy wasn't the same as it is today. As a kid you should please not disturb the grown-ups but find yourself something to play with quietly. Even better if it was outside and far away from the adults. We grew up in times of distrust and cynicism. The optimism of the 1950s and 1960s had drained out and hopelessness was growing in the 1970s and 1980s. The sexual revolution was replaced by the Aids crisis and the environment was heavily intoxicated.

The world was like a venue after a festival, littered, drained and waiting for somebody to clean up the mess. In the late 1970 and 1980s divorces sky-rocked in the US and many women joined the work force again. That's why many kids came home after school and stayed alone until dinner. The term "latchkey kids" was used to describe children wearing their door-key securely fastened to a chain worn around their necks. They came home and took care of themselves until their parents came back from work.

We grew up on our own, self-sufficient and independent. Nobody entertained us. We had to be creative otherwise life was pretty boring. In school nobody would defend us against bullies or injustice by teachers. It was "just the way it was" and we couldn't do much about it. We've also been called the "Lost Generation".

The economic expansion had left a mountain of debts and we graduated into a recession in the 1990s, followed by 9/11 in 2001, the crisis of 2007/2008 and the wars in Iraq and Afghanistan. We were the first generation to have lousier jobs than our parents and do financially worse.

The Millennials

Also referred to as "Gen Y" and "Echo Boomers" due to major birth rates in the 1980s and 1990s and mostly children of Baby Boomers or early GenXers. Roughly born between the early 1980s and late 1990s were born into a world that had just drastically changed. The Berlin Wall had fallen and the Soviet Union collapsed, there was hope again for a new world and technology experienced an exponential growth.

Most of Millennials had a cellphone as teens and grew up with a computer in their home. Music became freely available on the internet starting by the invention of the MP3 format in 1993 and Napster 1999-2001. It was the first platform for sharing songs online for *free*. Life became faster with internet and emails. Parents now had converted into "helicopter parents" who pampered and guided their children along their path, praising them and paying attention to their every little step. That made Millennials very self-centered and confident.

They are used to speak up and say what's on their mind, challenge authorities and know their rights and demand respect. Sometimes they are referred to as "the *Me* generation" because they claim their rights. Most Millennials are confident with social media and like to share and comment contents. But on the other side many are social media depended, searching for validation, eager for "likes" and attention. Most are enthusiastic, ambitious and energetic.

Many are confident and want to make a difference in the world. Also for Millennials studying and getting a decent job was much harder than for Baby Boomers because also they graduated into a recession (2007/2008) leaving them with high student debts and a hard time to find a stable career or a decent payed job. They witnessed the first reality shows, 9/11, Desert Storm, Hurricane Katrina, same sex marriage in

2004, then the crisis of 2007 and the election of Obama 2008 who promised to address all their problems: debt, healthcare and the environment. The financial struggle and problems of Millennials are very similar to the GenXers' but their approach to life and solving problems is often very different. Many Millennials are parents of Generation Alpha, born after 2015.

Generation Z

Also refereed to as "the i-Generation", "Zoomers" or "Gen Tech". Born roughly between the mid-late 90s and around the early 2010s. Due to Forbes 1996-2010, (other sources report 1995-2015). They were the first Generation to grow up with cellphones, internet and modern technology. The "i" stands for "internet" which most are very comfortable with.

For this generation the internet is like an element of nature as if it had been there since the dawn of time. That's why they have a completely different approach to technology than the generations before. Most Gen Z are children of GenXers and very different from other generations in many aspects. They are very realistic about their abilities, use social medias for creating their own "tribes" and are aware of being part of a group.

Most grew up after 9/11 and were young children in the recession of 2007/2008 so they have witnessed the financial struggle of their parents and families. The Economist has described them in an article of 02/27/2019 as *"more educated, well-behaved, stressed and depressed generation"* in comparison to the previous ones. Top reasons for feeling anxiety is reported to be money, school and social media. The great recession has led Gen Z to be entrepreneurial, independent and financially pragmatic. They represent the most ethnically diverse Generation in the US yet. A multi-culture, digitized and thoughtful cohort, demanding for new technology with different needs, they love shopping online and the market has to adapt to meet their standards. According to the US-Census-Bureau they only make up a quarter of the US population in 2015 outnumbered by Baby Boomers and Millennials.

So why haven't I heard of Gen X before?

There are many reasons for this, first of all we are a quite small demographic group compared to the others. Due to a narrower time span (15 years instead of 20) and lower birth-rates following the introduction of the birth control pill in 1964 and abortion legalization in the early 1970s. Immigration on the other hand made up for some of the gap and has contributed to make Gen X the *first* Generation to be ethnically diverse.

The other reason is, that were born between two very self-centered and demanding generations: the Baby Boomers and the Millennials. Generation X just happens to be the forgotten middle child. The other generations are too busy to fight each other to even notice us. But we are accustomed to that.

GenXers have *never* been in the center of attention.

Now we are all in our forties and early 50s but we still don't have a real name. In France we are called "Generation *Bof*"-, where "bof" could be translated as "whatever".

In his homonymous book, published in 2000, the German author Florian Illies calls us "Generation Golf" which apparently is the kind of car by Volkswagen that this generation could be represented by.

And that's about it. Until today nobody even knows who we are. Even most GenXers themselves don't know which generation they belong to.

Lack of a name leads to lack of identity.

We have grown into independent, patient and self-sufficient individuals very early. We are pragmatic and do our own thing. That is one more reason why we are so prickly about being identified as a generation at all.

Not having a real name or identity makes us still face prejudice from the other generations, Baby Boomers and Millennials who don't even know what generation we belong to either.

Usually they put us in the opposite cohort, with Boomers calling us Millennials and Millennials calling us Boomers.

But don't you dare "OK Boomer" *US*!

We've been dealing with them for more than 40 years already, welcome to the club!

("OK Boomer" is a 2019 Tik Tok song by Peter Kuli and interpreted by Jed Will, about Zoomers against Boomers).

We are a Generation of our *own*. We have our *own* story and the right to be here as well. Even if it amuses us a lot watching the other counterparts fight.

As long as they leave us out of their silly games...

5. X-TREME SPORTS

Growing up in the 1970s meant to be left often without any parental supervision in the afternoon. Childcare options outside home hadn't been invented yet, so we took care of ourselves and grew up very independent and responsible quite fast. We spend our time alone with our friends, playing, inventing new challenges and creating things. We were free to wander off and come home when the sun went down.

The adults often had no idea what we were doing but that was perfectly fine for us. No adult supervision, no questions, just freedom. We played outside with our bikes and built ramps on our own. Created tree-houses in the woods, played on the streets, in abandoned buildings and sneaked into ncighbor's barns.

The clothes for playing were be all ripped and dirty, we had our knees and elbows bruised and scratched and we always tried to improve our inventions or create new things. Most projects failed miserably but the process was always lots of fun. We tried to take our toys, bikes and skateboards apart and assemble them back together. Some screws always happened to remain left out in the end with either *no* or *disastrous* results for the vehicle. Either it worked anyway or the wheel fell of when we tried to jump the ramp. Our results were immediate, when we screwed up, it hurt really bad. When pieces broke off, we fixed or painted the item until they fell apart completely.

We were full of imagination and the world was our playground. We invented our own games and tried very dangerous things, watching each other's back in case somebody got injured. We jumped off rooftops, raced with shopping carts in a parking lot and let off firecrackers almost everywhere.

Shops were only allowed to sell them on December 31st, so we bought tons of them on New Years Eve and then blew them up all year long. Lit them in self built traps, old toys, snow, sand and plants. (corn has high, exposed roots and flies really high when you light a big firecracker at its base!) but don't try this at home – please!

Pretty dangerous stuff, I still wonder how we managed not to die all the time. We did get hurt though. Most of my friends had lost a tooth at some point, I broke off my front tooth at 8 years of age running up a metal slide from the wrong end. Another friend of mine tried to ride his skateboard downhill lying belly down on the board, facing forward. Front teeth gone.

Others broke their limbs, both of my sisters broke their arms at a certain point, but than we carried on playing the same games with a cast.

Nothing would stop us. Luckily we had the door key if we came home and nobody was there. If somebody got hurt we better hid it away from our parents otherwise they'd "give us the rest". Without adults watching and nobody giving us the idea of "danger" we pushed each other all the time to do crazier things. Skateboards and BMX bikes were very popular in the 80's and we built our own ramps to jump higher and try new stunts. We invented lots of challenges to "proof our courage" but it wasn't about munching tide pods (very popular sport among Gen Z in 2020 as you might know) but more about the adrenaline kick than about damaging our health.

That's how we grew into independent, fearless and patient thinkers. If there was a problem nobody would resolve it for us. We had to do it on our own, or it just wouldn't happen.

Complaining and crying wouldn't lead to anything. If the skateboard ramp that we had built, would collapse, we had to built a stronger one. If we crashed on our bike we had to get up and try again and again until we succeeded. If we did something wrong it was our own fault and responsibility.

One time we had built the coolest ramp for our bikes, out of mud and some wooden planks, which we thought was the best in the world. We all cheered our first friend trying the ramp for the first time.

He pushed the pedals to their limits and arrived at a very high speed. The wheel of his bike hit the ramp in the worst angle, the wooden plank flew away, re-bounced on the hill and was catapulted right back into his face. Luckily nothing terrible had happened but it was just the funniest slapstick scene ever. We burst into tears laughing. Then we made some modifications to the ramp and tried again. That's how we've become tough, responsible and auto sufficient.

There was not much dialogue between us and the gown-ups about our playing outside, we pretty much kept it all to ourselves. Our generation wouldn't rely too much on *anybody*, we made up our own rules and we are pretty confident about what we can and what we can't do, because we know our limits. We have tested them in real life.

Since we were creative, we started to invent more and more games, recreated something we had seen on TV, like in action movies. After some time they had added a voice that warned: "don't try this at home" but obviously we didn't listen to that. We even took it as a challenge

"They said don't try this at home"

"Great, let's try it"!

GenXers are innovative and fearless, we like to test our limits. So some of us started doing really dangerous things. In the early 1990s extreme sports had an exponential growth. Bungee-jumping, skateboarding, snowboarding and anything that might kill or injure somebody became very popular. In 1995 the first 'X Games' (Extreme Sport Games) were held in Newport, Providence, Mount Snow and Vermont in the US.

In 1994 MTV started airing "Wayne's World" starring Mike Myers and Dana Carvey pretending to be young adults hosting their own rock show in their parents basement. They presented new "extreme"-sports every now and then. Everything had become *extreme* from "extreme-toasting" (inserting nude hands inside a toaster) to "extreme-couch fishing" (searching for lost pieces of old pizza inside of their couch.) They were making fun of all the extreme sports that had become popular in that period. It was only a parody but, as parodies always do, reflected the trend of those years.

In the early 2000 a group of GenXers became famous on an MTV show called "Jackass", created by Jeff Tremaine, Johnny Knoxville and Spike Jonze. The contestants: Steve-O (1974), Johnny Knoxville (1971), Ryan Dunn (1977), Bam Margera (1979) and Jason 'Wee Man' Acuna (1973) – all actors and stuntmen - deliberately did all kinds of dangerous and painful tasks, just to test their limits.

We loved the show because they continued to do what we had started as kids. Of course they went overboard and did ridiculously crazy things that had nothing to do with sports.

They knew it was pointless to shoot a small cactus with a small canon at each other in a library at their naked torso, but we all loved to see them doing it, just to find out what would happen. We loved experiments and invented new things all the time.

But drinking shots of hot wax is pretty much like eating Tide pods. Way to dangerous. So sorry for you, Gen Z but you didn't invent a new trend at all. It was just crazy people doing crazy stuff to themselves or each other, just for the fun of it.

Some things were so extreme that even *we* wouldn't copy them. At a certain point some contestants' lives were destroyed by the show, due to injuries, car crashes, alcohol and drug abuse and even death.

Always living on the edge.

Even today in many extreme sports you will find a lot of GenXers having great fun testing their limits. In competitions you often see ambitious 20 year-old that are looking for the thrill of winning.

GenXers are less eager to win prizes, but focus on have fun while doing their sports. Also without competing against anybody and even when nobody sees them practicing.

It's a personal challenge, against themselves. Testing one's own limit. Most Iron men, Mountain-climbers and even the skydiver Felix Baumgartner (1969), who jumped from 39000 meters out of the stratosphere in a pressure suit to fall and parachute back to earth, are GenXers.

We don't care too much about what the others think. We just do it for the sake of it, for ourselves and for fun!

Most extreme sports are not team sports, but everybody on his own. Like Kite-surf, Wing-Suit-Flying, Base-Jumping, and Snow-board.

Us against ourselves and nature.

Extreme Sports = X-Sports.

Like us GenXers, independent, fearless and active.

Nobody can stop us.

6. TELEVISION

Whereas our parents as kids were *listening* to the radio or a bed time story read by a real person, we instead grew up *watching TV.*

It was often used as a pacifier, to calm us down or to make us stay quiet, the same way tablets and smart phones are used today to keep small kids busy. So instead of growing up on *words* we grew up on *images. Moving* images.

Millennials already had specific children's shows and many had access to internet they could interact with. Gen Z had YouTube and Social Media with the introduction of WiFi. Generation Alpha grew up directly using smartphones. But for us it was one-way communication.

Watching TV.

Since our parents were raised on *words* when they are under stress they like to *talk* to somebody or *listen* to soothing *words* to calm them down. Millennials reach out to social media to relax and Gen Z under stress spend some time on their smartphone. And Gen X? We don't believe much in words, they have never resolved any of our problems. We like *images*. Movies and series are our happy place. When we are stressed out and just want to relax we like to watch some TV to chill. That's different for every generation. This is another reason why we have trouble understanding each other.

Each age group has different needs, especially when they feel stressed. Baby Boomers need to *talk to relax* and they feel that if you never *talk* you cannot relax. That stresses out the other generations like GenXers who just want to *watch* a movie and younger Generations who prefer spend some time alone on their phone.

In the 1970s and 1980s there was no "children's channel" not even a single one. Merely 3 or 4 normal channels totally to choose from, on analog TV.

Between 2am and 6am there were no transmissions at all, but if you switched on the TV anyway (of course we tried that, too!) we only saw a bright colored pattern, called 'the test card' introduced in 1967 on BBC2. The sound was an intense, steady tone in various pitches.

Sometimes at the end of transmission there was only *white noise.* Black and white points flicking around like crazy accompanied by a terrible static noise. In some countries the random pixel pattern was referred to as 'snow', in others 'bugs' or 'war of the ants'.

The antenna in that moment picks up all electronic noise and radio-waves from the surrounding area and displays it on the screen. The thermal and transistor noise is heard in the accompanying sound. We believed to capture "ghost" conversations or paranormal phenomenon by recording this white noise. That idea surely was amplified by the movie

"Poltergeist" by Steven Spielberg from 1982 where the young protagonist communicates with ghosts though the white noise on TV. Tragically four of the main actors died under mysterious circumstances after the trilogy was published, including the protagonist.

It is considered to be the most cursed movie in Hollywood. So we decided to avoid the white noise and switch the TV off after 'end of transmission'. Just in case.

In the early 1970s some televisions were still in black and white and we also watched some old movies from the 1950s and 1960s that were transmitted in black and white anyway.

Then, in the 1980s, most households had *one* color TV for the *whole* family (remember no computers or internet yet for another 15 years). It was a heavy, square box and cats would love to sleep on top of it because it was so large and warm. The TV was usually placed in the living room and became part of the family. Sometimes in the morning or afternoon there was a special children's program but only for 25 minutes per episode.

That's why we grew mainly up on adult movies and series. In the 1980s the TV-series Magnum PI (80-88), Night Rider (82-86), Miami Vice (84-90) and Remington Steele (82-87) were very popular, always glamorous looking people solving crimes.

Then there was the A-team (83-87), Simon&Simon (81-89), Riptide (83-86), Hart to Hart (79-84) and lots of other TV- series. They all had one thing in common: the pictures and the action was important, but dialogue was left behind. They would always fight in the end to get the bad guys.

Many cult movies of the 1980s, like Top Gun (1986), Rambo (1982, 1985, 1988) and Terminator (1984) were based on pictures, sounds and special effects. So we grew up wanting to be as cool as Tom Cruise or Bruce Willis.

At playtime we recreated the movies with our toys, making explosion sounds and noises, no dialogue required. We didn't get to grow up listening to able speakers expressing themselves in fancy sentences or long motivation monologues. Only some catch phrase and most likely and explosion in the end.

Like "hasta la vista, babe" or "I'll be back" in the movie "Terminator 2". We loved those movies and that feeling of power that came with them. We didn't just *watch* the movie, we bought the whole *soundtrack*. The soundtrack of the movie "Terminator 2" in 1991 was even produced by Guns 'n Roses! "You could be mine" - Great stuff!.

We listened to the music and tried to dress, act and speak as our favorite movie characters. Which Gen X-boy hasn't played "Rambo" as a kid?

With the first video tapes, VHS and Beta Gen X were the first to could enjoy "home cinema". We often went to the "Blockbuster" store 1985-2013 to rent movies on VHS and later on DVDs and that was not cheap at all. Sometimes our parents got us a VHS tape as a gift on Christmas and we would watch the same movie over and over again.

Obviously the experience of seeing a movie in a real cinema is completely different, the screen is much bigger and more impressive than a small box at home. On the other hand the experience also stays in the theater. When you have videotapes and can watch a movie over and over again in your home, it becomes part of your life, the characters become family. You get all the small details, the catchphrases and the little hints. We watched all the cartoons by Walt Disney, some special children's movies like "Pippi Longstocking from 1969" - she was home alone as well - and some old funny movies our parents introduced us to.

Then we grew older and started watching *horror* movies. The world was very hostile towards children in the 1970s and that even reflects in the movies of that time. Birth-rates had dropped rapidly from 1961 until 1975 to hit a low in 1976. With new possibilities (birth control pill and abortion legalization) it became OK *not* to want any children.

That's why horror movies in the 1970s had created a new genre, the *"child devil"* as in "The exorcist" (1973) or "The Omen" (1976) stating openly for the first time the believe that children were *evil*.

"Rosemary's baby"(1968) by Roman Polànski was the predecessor of this idea. The year 1966 was considered to be "666-the year of beast" as predicted by "the new testament's book of revelation" and in many movies the newborn turned out to be Satan's offspring. Surprise! The Devil's son is a GenXer! All 'Lucifans' knew that already. (Fans of the series "Lucifer" on Netflix).

Children were not very welcome in many places and we saw and felt that even though watching movies.

On November, 18th in 1978 in Jones town, Guyana, 913 members of "Peoples Temple" committed the largest mass suicide in American history at behest of their leader Jim Jones. A fruit drink laced with cyanide was given to drink to the cult members. Over 300 victims were 17 and under. I remember playing in our garden with my sisters, throwing all kinds of poisonous plants together in a small bucket and stirring around. When our parents asked us what we were doing we replied *"preparing poison for children"*.

Also on Halloween some crazy people had prepared chocolate snacks with blades for kids. It was dark place to grow up in.

Then our generation finally grew old enough to have their own movies: GenX-movies treating GenX-topics with GenX-actors. Most stories were about young kids who resolved their problems on their own:

"The Goonies" (1985) introduces us to the adventure of a group of young teenagers. They try to save their homes by following a treasure map and finding a lost pirate ship with its treasure. They have to use their creativity, each single one's special talent, like translating, playing the piano and team work to complete the task. The only real threat is the "Fratelli Family" - the adults who want to steal their treasure.

We loved that movie and we were obsessed about the idea of going on an adventure, only us kids, saving the world. We designed treasure maps, went on adventure trips and dreamed of being the heroes of the world.

In "Stand By Me" (1986) a group of four teenagers leave for a 2 day-hike to search for their deceased school mate without telling their parents. No grown ups, all the responsibilities are on them. They even got away without anybody even wondering were they were, without cell phones, in the woods, at 12/13 years of age. That would be impossible nowadays. I loved that movie, it is all about trust and friendship, sticking together, no matter what. It also underlines the fact of how dangerous the world was we were growing up in. A 12-year-old was dead in the woods and nobody came to search for him. We knew about child abductions, missing children on milk containers and really creepy people out there. Also in "Stand by me" the only real danger is represented by the young adults that arrive by car and threaten the four.

We learned to mistrust adults and read people's intentions very quickly. From an early age we were told not to "accept chocolate from strangers" (it could be poisoned) and never get into a stranger's car. Just follow those two rules and you will be fine. Cool!

Our parents had been hitch-hiking happily for decades but for us that was never an option. Death was a daily threat we could have faced if we wouldn't have acted responsibly.

Also in " Kevin Home Alone" (1990) a 10 year-old kid was forgotten at home by his parents. Luckily he knew how to use his creativity to defend himself and his parent's house against two clumsy thieves.

The problem was never that the children were *alone* in those movies. It was always created by adults who wanted to *harm* the kids - and they had to defend themselves. Also Pippi Longstocking had to be strong to defend her father's treasure on her own against sneaky thieves. Luckily she had super powers.

Then other films were produced that talked about growing up in the 1980s and facing school, the system and society:

In 1985 "the Breakfast Club" was released, a movie about 5 adolescence in detention a whole Saturday at school. Just sitting there and being punished for different reasons. It was the first movie about young adult GenXers (born in the late 1960s). From different backgrounds and social levels they all agree on one fact: they *don't* want to become like their parents. In one scene Claire, one of the students, states: *"Either way they don't give a shit. I hope we don't become like our parents..."* but Allison, the other girl, replies: *"It's unenviable, because when you grow up your heart dies".*

They say that GenXers are *reluctant* to grow up. If by "growing up" they intend becoming like your parents, they are 100% right. There is a good reason for this. Throughout the movie we learn about parents that are not satisfied with their offspring, they humiliate them because of the parents' "zero tolerance against losers" and are not happy with them being "weak".

That's exactly the point. We *do* care for others, for others' feelings, we don't want to carry on that endless battle of winners and losers, we don't believe in a society where one humiliates the other.

Being kind is not a bad thing and having feelings neither. But the Baby Boomer generation was raised in a different way. They got attacked as kids and could fight back. We instead were told to be *good* and *caring* and afterwards were humiliated by teachers and society for being what in their eyes is "weak".

For us being nice and caring *is* being strong. It is much harder to be nice and helping others than to be mean. It takes courage. But they will never get it. They are so used to attacking everybody right away that they did the same even to their own children.

In another scene from "the Breakfast Club" Andrew, the sports student, tells the others the reason for him being in detention. To please his father, who constantly brags about all the crazy things he used to do in college, he had put tape around the butt of a weaker boy in the changing room.

His father is proud of this action, but Andrew is devastated by the thought of what that boy must have gone through going back to his home and being humiliated by his parents. He feels very sorry for his victim.

Self doubt and trying to put oneself in other people's shoes is a concept that the generations before didn't adopt. The teenagers in the movie are taught to write an essay about themselves, but in the end they decide to just write one page altogether, addressing directly their Baby Boomer teacher, Mr Vernon:

"Dear Mr Vernon, You see us the way you want to see us, in the the simplest terms and the most convenient definitions"

Which can be translated into "you don't know even who we are and you're not interested in getting to know us.

You judge us right away because that's convenient for you. So we don't even bother to write about us, it would be useless."

Other famous GenXer movies of the 80s are:

"Ferris Bueller's Day Off" (1986) with Matthew Broderick, Mia Sara, Jennifer Grey and Charlie Sheen and "Say anything" (1989) with John Cusack and Ione Skye

In the early 90 we saw movies about the early GenXers in their 20s, young adults trying to figure out how to live on their own, without getting married or start a family.

A concept that had never existed before: our grandparents and parents had left their family only the moment they got married. Hardly anybody had lived on their own, trying to figure out life, struggle to find a decent job or built a relationship.

These were all new questions that nobody had the answer to. So the film industry came up with new topics in the Gen X-movies of the 90s:

"Singles" (1992) with Bridget Fonda, Campbell Scott, Kyra Sedgwick and Matt Dillon

"Reality bites" (1994), with Wiona Ryder, Ethan Hawke and Ben Stiller

"Four Weddings and a Funeral" (1994) Starring Andy McDowell, Hugh Grant and John Hannah

"Picture Perfect" (1997) with Jennifer Aniston and Kevin Bacon and Jay Mohr

"Sliding Doors (1998) with Gwyneth Paltrow and John Hannah

"You've got mail" (1998) starring Meg Ryan and Tom Hanks

"There's something about Mary" (1998) starring Cameron Diaz, Ben Stiller and Matt Dillon

"Notting Hill" (1999) with Julia Roberts and Hugh Grant

These movies all introduce us to young adults living with their roommates or by themselves. They all deal with challenges of Gen X in modern society, like their career and lifestyle choices. Confronting us with new situations nobody had faced yet.

I remember the mood of my generation in the 90s, we were young and had to decide what to do with our lives. Our parents had already been married in their early 20s and had children at a very young age. But that's not what most of us wanted or could afford. We had always been told what we were supposed to be doing, as all generations, but in our heads we had decided to simply oppose ourselves and *not* do the expected.

For me one of the most expressive GenX movies of the 1990s is trainspotting (1996) directed by Danny Boyle, based on the 1993 novel by Irvine Welsh.

Showing mostly GenXers,

Mark - Ewan McGregor 1971
Sick Boy - Johnny Lee Miller 1972,
Spud - Ewen Bremner 1972,
Diane - Kelly McDonald 1976
Gail - Shirley Henderson 1965
Tommy - Kevin McKidd 1973
Francis – Robert Carlyle 1961

in their early 20s addressing the struggle of finding a purpose in life.

In the first scene we hear Mark's Voice claiming:

"Choose life, choose a job, choose a career. Choose a family, choose a fucking big television, choose washing

machines, cars, compact disc players and electrical tin openers, choose good health, low cholesterol and dental insurance. Choose fixed interest mortgage payments, choose a starter home, choose your friends, choose leisurewear and matching luggage.

Choose a tree piece suit on hire purchase in a range of fucking fabrics. Choose DIY and wondering who the fuck are you on Monday morning, choose sitting on that couch watching mind numbing spirit crushing game shows, stuffing fucking junk food into your mouth,

Choose rotting away at the end of it all pissing your last in a miserable home nothing more than an embarrassment to the selfish fucked up brats you spawned to replace yourselves. Choose your future, choose life. But why would I want to do a thing like that? I chose not to choose life, I chose something else. And the reason? There are no reasons. Who needs reasons when you've got heroin?" (Trainspotting 1996).

This is actually a reaction to the anti drug campaign in the 90, "say no to drugs, say yes to life". The response is cynical and realistic: so you want me to choose "Life"? what do you mean by "Life"? Do you think that this is better because I fit in this rat-race, working and consuming and becoming numb and brain dead? When you say "choose Life" you mean *"choose what I have planned for you to be, another slave in this society, working all day to by stuff and having no real meaning in life?"* I might as well say yes to drugs.

The most important phrase is: " I *chose* something else" Whatever it is that you *don't* tell me to do.

The Baby Boomers had created their own world after

WWII and now we were supposed to accept it as it was and live by *their* rules? No! A big no. I chose *not* to choose "the life" you have in mind for me, I want to choose my *own* life. The slogan "no future" was a punk orientated music label of the 1980s and expressed the same idea. "We see no future for ourselves, not a future that seems worth living".

We had no idea what our life was going to be like. Nobody had ever lived a life similar to ours before. We explored new terrain and had no clue what to do. But we knew exactly what we *didn't* want to do and that kept us going.

In the 1990s many new cult films were released that we still refer to in our daily lives:

"Jurassic Park" (1993) by Steven Spielberg made us wonder if we would have 'mini dinosaur pets' in the future or could clone a dead celebrity back to life. The possibilities seemed endless and the whole idea of 'cloning' stuck in our heads and caused many ethic controversies and debates. Only 2 years later, in 1996, the sheep Dolly was cloned.

"Forrest Gump" (1994) with Tom Hanks is a classic that takes us through recent history (from the 1960s to the 1990s) and has been quoted ever since like: *"Mama always said life was like a box of chocolate, you never know what you're gonna get"* and *"stupid is as stupid does"* which means that everybody should be judged on their actions and not on their appearance.

"Pulp Fiction" (1994) and "From dusk to dawn" (1996) by Quentin Tarantino - like all his movies - wrote cinematographic history by twisting the plot and creating epic dialogues .

"Titanic" (1997) starring Leonardo DiCaprio and Kate Winslet used computer technology and green screen to create a whole ship *" I am the king of the world"* and *"the whistle scene"* have been copied in parodies, and movies all over the world. Besides that, we all know, that there was space for two on that door, there are even reconstructions on the internet to prove that!

"Men in Black" (1997) with Will Smith and Tommy Lee Jones was yet another fun way of telling us that our whole existence was a lie and that in reality mankind had lived together with aliens from the beginning of time

"The Truman Show" (1998) with Jim Carrey reminds of the plot from "Nineteen Eighty-Four" published by George Orwell in 1949. The movie introduced us to the protagonist who unknowingly lives in a fake world under surveillance cameras for pure entertainment purposes. It came to cinemas when first reality show were introduced on TV (Big Brother 1997) and started a discussion about boundaries for the entertainment industry.

"The Fight Club" (1999) starring Brad Pitt and Edward Norton didn't meet the expectations at the box office but became a cult with its release on DVD.

"The Matrix" (1999) staring Keanu Reeves introduced us to a future where humans lived enslaved, without being conscious about their situation, attached to machines. Created by a cyber intelligence that lives of the humans' body energy and imprison their minds within an artificial reality called "the matrix" .

That movie blew our minds and made everybody think about their existence. The internet had just become part of our lives some years earlier, so we were faced with the risk that an artificial intelligence could enslave us in the future. There had been other movies like "War games" (1983), "Terminator" (1984) and "RoboCop"(1987) about robots destroying our lives but this was something very different. In all the other movies the humans were conscious about what was going on and could fight to win back their freedom.

In "the Matrix" the humans were unaware of what was happening. They just lived their normal lives in their heads whereas their bodies were drained of their vital energy and later disposed of as empty batteries.

Many movies released in the 1990s were about our existence, aliens and robots and the makers tried to invent new and creative ideas to make us reconsider everything we knew about life, ethics and philosophy. What was right or wrong: cloning living beings or allowing cyber intelligence decide about our lives. It made us dream and think about new possibilities and scenarios, life in the future could be fantastic again.

But then the reality was different. The stock markets crashed, the crisis hit and now it's all about money. All the discussions, protests, decisions. Even when we talk about the environment or health. It's all calculations, debt and economy. No more ideologies, future plans. Now after the Covid-19 lock down I am sure it will be even worse.

Later, in the 2000s we saw lots of other movies, about GenXers in their thirties:

In 2001 "Bridget Jones's Diary" was released. Based on the columns and novel by the British writer Helen Fielding we meet Bridget, a 32 year old single who tries to make sense of life and relationships, with the help of her friends. The great success of this book and movie is explained by the character which we all can relate to.

Her parents are divorced with their own problems. Bridget tries to help them and make the right choices in life which she often fails at. Also the two male characters are typical GenXers in their thirties: Daniel, her boss never seems to want to commit to a serious relationship and Mark who is trying to be kind and gentle but doesn't get through to Bridget either.

To help her in her decisions are not her parents but her friends. As we often see in these movies or sitcoms, friends in GenXers lives are our "surrogate family", we help each other in any situation, we've got each others back and nobody knows us like our friends do. That has replaced the traditional "family"of previous generations where people would seek advice and shelter.

Maybe "Bridget Jones's Diary" has been a great success because we all know the characters of this movie in our real lives. We all know a "Daniel"-type man, the adult with a "Peter Pan" syndrome who never is going to commit to any woman because he can just have them all. Similar to the "Barney" character in "How I met your mother". Some girls still think that maybe he just needs the right woman to fall in love and then he will change. Yes, right LOL.

On the other hand there is Mark, a very intelligent, highly educated, polite and gentle person who nobody seems to fall for. Love is indeed complicated. It is a tribute to the singles in the world.

In 2000 Generation X has also been also called "the Friends- generation" (as the sitcom "F.R.I.E.N.D.S" 1994-2004). *"Aimless but fun"*. Because many in our 30s still were neither married nor had kids. That was terrible for Baby Boomers to witness. For them it was a useless life and we had no goals nor perspective. Even the protagonists were very ambitious, motivated and anti-establishment. But that wasn't good enough. Of course. In 2020, a quarter century later, many Millennials and Gen Z love to watch "F.R.I.E.N.D.S" on Netflix. That's about *our* generation, folks. Even if you might not like that idea.

Movies today in 2020 are often either biographic or documentaries. We are on a quest for the truth, want the plot to be as realistic as possible and without old taboos. Nobody is 'safe', there are movies, series and documentaries about all forbidden topics: church, politics and conspiracy theories.

It's like reading the newspaper, we want to get to the bottom of our problems and discover long held secrets. Since Wikileaks, the Panama Papers and Edward Snowden who revealed massive surveillance by the CIA we are demanding for the truth. No more fiction or future plans but understanding our history and present.

In 2019 besides "Bohemian Rhapsody" another film was released that automatically fascinated the audience. The remake of this famous character was much darker and deeper than any version before:

"Joker" starring Joaquin Phoenix

He wasn't the usual 'bad boy' as in previous versions. This Joker was deeply troubled and sad. Watching the movie I couldn't help but realize, it could be the story of an unfortunate GenXer in modern society.

Of course you might disagree, surely not all GenXers have failed in life and society. That's not the point. I will take you through some scenes of the film and explain you where I see the connection. We all know people struggling with life, finances and their job and a similar story to tell.

Based on a Comic book some concepts are exaggerated. But if you take a closer look, some scenes seem very familiar. Don't worry, I will not reveal too many details to whom hasn't watched it yet.

Arthur, a single in his 40s, works as a street clown and lives with his sick mother whom he takes care off. He feels embarrassed by a syndrome that makes him laugh in odd moments. Just in case he carries around small paper notes for apologizing to people he might disturb with his inappropriate laughter.

He doesn't want to annoy people and apologizes for his syndrome even if it's not his fault. Growing up he had been lied to and neglected by his mother. He never met his father and is told a different story every time about his origins. His mother suffers from dementia and mental illness. They live in poverty and food is never enough so he remains starving leaving his part to her.

At work he gets bullied and attacked by teenagers who steal his cardboard sign and beat him up just for the fun of it. They don't care if he is working hard to earn some money and feed his mother. Also his boss doesn't even listen to his version but detracts the money for the board from his paycheck.

When he tries to talk to the person who he thinks could be his father in a very humble way, that man gets very upset, abuses him verbally and punches him in the face.

He stumbles through life, trying to be nice to people and make them smile but all he receives is verbal and physical abuse by the younger and the elder. Even when he gets provoked, he walks the other way until his opponents leave him no other choice.

One evening some young rich people mock him on the train and beat him up, until he has to fight back to defend himself. Overnight he becomes anonymously famous but still doesn't take the credit for it, even if now he is a legend for standing up for the poor people.

He just wants some recognition for taking care of his mother all by himself by a TV host he watches all the time. But that TV host is a very selfish, self entitled person impersonated by Robert De Niro. He doesn't care for what Arthur is going through, he invites him to his show to publicly humiliate him for his syndrome.

We can all now relate to this character, he has been trying to be humble all the time, cares for his mother, even if she had mistreated him, works under difficult circumstances for a ridiculous wage, takes the bullying and tries to find his father. But he just receives mockery, is assaulted and laughed at. Now he is fed up.

He prepares for his appearance on the TV show and the things he want to say. He knows that the host is not going to listen to him, but he prepares a speech anyway. So when the great day comes and he tries to speak, the host (as expected) starts mocking him right away and lectures him about life and what is right or wrong. We have seen this scene over and over in our lives. We have something important to say but again some Baby Boomer knows it all better, they don't listen to any argument and are not able to dialogue. Just endless lectures and monologues. How many times have we been through this? Endless.

But this time Arthur is fed up. He has something to say to and wants everybody to listen. He takes a deep breath and claims:

"In this system that knows so much you decide whats right or wrong the same way decide whats funny or not. Everybody is awful these days. Its enough to make everybody crazy. Nobody is civil anymore"...

"Have you seem whats it's like out there? Everybody just yells and screams at each other. Nobody thinks what it's like to be the other guy"...

"What do you get.. when you cross a mentally ill loner... with a society that abandons him and treats him like trash? You get what you fuckin' deserve!"

Then he walks away without even trying to lecture everybody or to make people understand. Because he knows that they won't get it. They don't care.

We as GenXers can relate to his feelings and understand why he got where he is now. We have been humiliated and downplayed our feelings but when we said we had enough they said we were pitying ourselves.

Standing up for one's rights and pointing out that someone is treating us wrong shouldn't be called *self pity*. Because it is not. You wouldn't tell a bullied child today to not feel 'self pity'. But our generation has always been told exactly that.

The same thing that "Claire" (Molly Ringwald) in "The Breakfast Club" pointed out, answering the question:

"why do you pity yourself"

with:

"Because If I wouldn't nobody would..."
"I'm tired of pretending".

Millennials were told to express themselves and parents payed attention not to hurt their children's feelings. But for us, when we were angry, sad or troubled about something we always heard "don't pity yourself". End of story. Nobody took your defense against any injustice.

When I was in high school there was the opportunity to get selected for a trip to Dallas. Everybody would stay in a family as an exchange student for a week and then the other pupils would come to our house. I really wanted to go and was thrilled about the idea.

They interviewed all our teachers if we were good students and could fit into a family. When the list of the names was published I was the first one to arrive at school. But my name wasn't on it. My class teacher had decided that I was not fit for a family since I *was a girl and I would say out loud if disagreed to something".*

I was devastated. There were some boys on the list who always criticized everything, but they were *boys*. Boys were allowed to do that. I tried to talk to the teachers but that didn't change anything. My parents never talked to the teachers, I had to deal with it and forget about it. *"Don't pity yourself, there are many kids that don't get to go"*. But that has nothing to do with self pity. It's injustice.

But since there was no justice and we got punished every time we tried to speak up, most of us shut down. Became cynical with a deep distrust in the system and society. Then they called us *slackers*.

Also Arthur in "the Joker" isn't "pitying" himself, as the TV host says, but pointing out what's wrong in society. People are yelling and screaming at each other without even trying to understand. That's exactly what happens to Gen X who didn't follow Baby Boomers' society rules but stayed on their own path.

We believed in treating people with kindness and respect, being humble and patient. But in real life, when we behave like this, we get mistreated, exploited and laughed at. That's why I am convinced that this is a movie about us. *'We are all clowns'*.

At some point we had to eventually comply to society rules, be aggressive from time to time, stand up for ourselves, demand respect and defend our rights. Like Arthur says: *"Someday somebody will break you so badly that you will become unbreakable"*.

He knows about his mental illness and seeks help from a social advisor. But public money is short so they close the facility. He looses the only person that had listened to him at *all*. He is very disappointed, angry and bitter from being mistreated and abandoned although he has done nothing but being kind in life.

We know that justice often is not served at all and we have a deep mistrust in the system. During the movie we are introduced to his life, it could be easily the story of a real person in today's society.

He has never been given the chance to climb the ladder of success due to his illness. No matter how hard he tries to control his problems or earning some money to feed himself, society doesn't help him. Instead people take advantage of his condition and mock him. He just cannot take it anymore and says:

"The Mayor just thinks that we'll sit there and take it like good little boys? That we won't werewolf and go wild?"

We can all only take so much. So be careful, other Generations, don't mock us because you think we are weak. We are humble and kind. But we are also tough and patient. We don't explode in your face in rage but stay calm and focused to elaborate a plan to make you crumble.

Don't go too far. We can turn into werewolves. We have been accumulating offenses and humiliation for way too long.

And we don't need any backup. We are used to rely on nobody but *ourselves*. Each of us is stronger than you think.

You have no idea of what we are capable of.

7. SITCOMS

In the 1980s and 1990s sitcoms were very popular, like "the Cosby Show" (1984-1992), "the Fresh Prince of Bel-Air" (90-96), "ALF" (1986-1990), "the Hogan Family" (1986-1991), "As Long As We've Got Each other" (1985-1992) and "Married with children" (1987-1997), just to name a few. When you think, that the title "Married with children" was a little judging you should listen to the theme song that goes: *love and a marriage... you can't have one without the other*.

So much for psychological terror in the 1980s. They all showed traditional families, living perfectly together and facing everyday problems. Perfect Sitcoms to watch for children with divorced parents. Especially "Family Ties (1982-1989) or " Family Matters" (1989-1998).

Usually the father went to work, the mom stayed at home with the kids and all were perfectly happy. Everybody was always looking impeccable, with styled hair, modern clothes and always kind and neat.

When you grow watching this type of sitcoms and perceive them as the reality, you will often feel inadequate.

If your family was different that you didn't perceive yourself as 'normal'. You start doubting if maybe you're not good enough, not skinny or pretty, well enough dressed, surely not always perfect and happy. Yes, everybody was happy and smiling in these sitcoms all the time.

Even in the series "fame" (1983-1987) and "a different world"(1987-1993), where more serious topics were dealt with, everybody had amazing bodies, make up and style.

Everybody always made it.

There was no space for being different.

The early 1990s brought us "Beverly Hills 90210" (1990-2000), Melrose Place (1992-1999) and Dawson's Creek (1998-2003), all about teenagers and their problems growing up.

The first sitcom about young adults, leaving their family and sharing an apartment with their room mates in real life was "F.R.I.E.N.D.S." (1994-2004).

The cast members were all the first GenXers in their 20s
Jennifer Anniston (1969),
Courteney Cox (1965),
Matthew Perry (1969),
Lisa Kudrow (1963)
Matt Le Blanch (1967) and
David Schwimmer (1966).

It was a completely new concept after decades of showing only 'traditional' families on TV. The new 'family' wasn't Mom, Dad, siblings or cousins, but friends. Absolutely shocking. It was OK in college but for working adults to live with their *friends* was insane. The first

GenXers who had chosen this kind of lifestyle were mobbed by society and their families for not "fitting in". *'You don't want to marry and have kids? What is wrong with you?'*. They didn't consider a different type of lifestyle to be adequate.

Also in the sitcom "F.R.I.E.N.D.S." (1994-2004) everybody was skinny, perfectly dressed and very handsome. We found out only 25 years later that the protagonists have always been on a strict diet. "Jennifer had to lose 30 lbs to get the starring role" states Saul Austerlitz in his 2019 book 'Generation Friends'

Also Lisa Kudrow admitted on 'vogue.com', May 21st 2019, that she starved herself sick and was always underweight while on the show.

How were normal teenagers and young adults supposed to compete with that? Many suffered from eating disorders just like our movie stars. We were so fed up with perfect families, perfect bodies and perfect hair.

Luckily today we have new sitcoms, like "Two and a half men" (2003-2015), "Mike&Molly" (2010-2016) and "MOM" (2013-present). Written by Chuck Lorre/Warner Bros) which show different 'family' compositions.

In "Two and a half men" a divorced, broke father lives with his son at his brother's house. Mike, Molly and her sister in "Mike & Molly" still live with their divorced mothers and the protagonist of "MOM" is a working, single mother living with her two children and her mom.

Finally people can identify themselves with one of the new family types, they are all families and equally good.

Apart from this fact, all three sitcoms are so precise at describing GenXers real life, it's hilarious! I suppose that's why we find them so funny. They are deeply true.

Especially for the attitude their parents are bringing towards them. If you are familiar with these sitcoms you will immediately understand what I'm talking about: In "Two and a half men" the protagonists' mother is extremely wealthy but doesn't care for her sons. She hates them as much as they hate her back. Charlie (Charlie Sheen, 1965) is wealthy due to his creativity, he composes jingles. His brother Alan (John Cryer, 1965) is a divorced man who is always broke though he works all day as a chiropractor. Their mother instead lives in a beautiful villa, loves luxury and parties.

"Mike and Molly" are both working, but living with their parents because they cannot afford a flat. Mike (Billy Gardell 1969) is a police officer and Molly (Melissa Mc Carthy, 1970) a school teacher. Both have weight issues and meet at the Over Eaters Anonymous.

Their mothers are hilarious. Molly's mom downplays Molly and her sister all the time and often says she *would be better off without them.* 'I had kids because everybody had them'. When their father died, she neglected her kids even though she denies that. Showing no interest whatsoever in her daughters' lives she is busy with her own, drinking and partying. When we see Molly's childhood memories it's like going back in time: Every body wears bright colors and patterns, the adults smoke inside and drink and the kids try to perform something while nobody pays attention... the perfect scenario!

Mike was raised by his mother because his father left when he was a little boy. He still carries that feeling of being abandoned and shares this issue with Molly. To overcome their loss, both had started over eating. Now as adults they help each other coping with their issues. "Mike and Molly" also mixes ethnic groups. Mike's friend and colleague 'Carl' (Reno Wilson 1969) is African-American and lives alone with his grandmother. He's the type of guy that doesn't want to commit to a relationship and is happy the way things are going. Their friend "Samuel" (Nyabi Nyabi, 1979) is an African immigrant and makes fun of the culture differences.

Instead of being perfect, everybody has their issues, flaws and background. All shapes and sizes, people with real problems and issues. Packed into a sit-comedy, finally! Make the *situation* funny, not people's defects.

In "MOM" we meet a single working mother Christy (Anna Faris, 1976) living with her two kids. She has to handle her pregnant teenage daughter Violet (Sadie Calvano, 1997) and her broke mother Bonnie (Allison Janney, 1959) who also came to live with them. Christy was born when Bonnie was still a teenager and a drug addict. She has always had to take care of her mother, even as a child and things haven't changed much.

Christy runs the family all by herself, but instead of helping, her children and her own mom criticize everything all the time. Can anybody relate?

Finally sitcoms show the flaws, embarrassing moments and weaknesses of the characters. What people can relate to in real life. The failure, bad hair day or terrible fashion choices.

Also "the Big Bang Theory" (2007-2019) talks about late GenXers: Jim Parson (1973), Johnny Galecki (1975), Mayim Bialik (1975), Melissa Rauch (1980), Kunal Nayyar (1981) and Simon Helberg (1980). All in their late 30s and 40s but still sharing flats as friends, dressing and behaving like big boys and girls with comic T-Shirts and Hoodies. All doctors in very important positions they don't care for status symbols or showing off their money. They still live their lives as when they were college students.

Their next door neighbor is the younger Kaley Cuoco (1985) who is a Millennial, approaching life in a different way. But apart from her everybody is dressed in a casual way: Funny T-shirts, Hoodies and Jeans which are not perfect or attractive, but realistic. All parents of the main characters are more self-absorbed than caring and mostly make fun of their children instead of supporting them.

Also the sitcom "How I met your mother" (2005-2014) introduces us to the real life of GenXers, in their late 20s and 30s. All trying to find their way in life and figure out what they really want: Ted, Marshall and Lily try to be respectful, honest and caring for other people's feelings. Robin and Barney instead are two independent, lonely wolves who are used to do everything on their own. Without complaining or blaming anybody for their failure, always continue fighting to make their way in life, like most of us do.

All main characters have parent issues (perfectly self-centered Baby Boomers) who are more concerned of what *they* want from life than what their children are going through. Even now in their adult age. They are not even listening to their grown up children's questions or dilemmas because they are still busy with their own love life, career or interests. Four out of five parents of the characters are divorced and have never been there for their offspring as kids. The stories of young Robin and Barney make us laugh because we know exactly what they are talking about.

Barney had never met his Dad and his mother made up new stories everyday which he, as a young kid, obviously believed in. Robin's Dad, on the other hand, had always wanted a son and treats his daughter like one, not caring for her needs or feelings at all.

All five friends had to get through their lives on their own and could never count on their parents neither as kids nor as adults. That's why their group of friends is so crucial.

We've been fans of GenXers in movies for all our lives and it was very painful to see and hear that many child-stars were abused and exploited. The actor Corey Feldman who had been starring in "The Goonies", "Stand by me", "Lost boys" and many other movies has written a book about this dark side of Hollywood.

In his book "Coreyography: a memoir", published in 2013 he reveals the physical, sexual and drug abuse, that so many others of this generation were exposed to as young children. Many have been trapped in a cycle of self-destruction and drug abuse,as his friend Corey Haim who passed away in 2010.

It's a tale of survival and redemption.

Also songwriter Billy Corgan from the Smashing Pumpkins has written the song "disarm" about the abuse in his childhood. Some people say that they only seek for attention. No they don't. And they don't "pity" themselves either.

It takes a lot of courage and a long time to deal with the past and clean out one's closet. They have been silenced for too many years. Now it's time to listen to *them*.

8. NETFLIX

During Lock down most people really got into watching TV, movies and especially series. You've probably noticed that also the series on Netflix reflect our approach towards life, relationships, love and problems in general.

There is a variety of series for Gen Z, Millennials, Boomers and - guess what - GenXers. Gen X-actors addressing Gen X topics. Maybe that's why – unconsciously - we are drawn more towards one series than the other.

While one might seem absurd or we just don't understand why the characters behave in a certain way, we feel a deeper connection towards others and can relate more to the characters because they are more similar to us.

Some of the latest I have seen was "Lucifer", "the Good place" and "The After Life". All three are completely different from each other, but in a profound way they all deal with GenXer problems and lives. I won't spoil anything about the story but focus on the characters for a moment.

"Lucifer" is about the devil (Tom Ellis, 1978) coming to earth on holidays. He meets some police officers whom he starts working with. They are all in their 40s, some divorced with children and others are still looking for love, their true identity or meaning of life. Being celestial or human, the problems of all species seem to be very similar in the end.

Also in Lucifer we can see the classic gender roles of Generation X: The main female characters are all very strong, independent and devoted to their job, children and their dreams.

Chloe (Lauren German, 1978) is divorced, has a daughter and is very committed to her job ad a detective.

Linda (Rachel Harris, 1968) is a divorced, independent woman, working as a psychoanalyst.

Maze (Lesley-Ann Brandt, 1981) is a demon who is extremely strong, loves to fight and her sexuality.

Charlotte (Tricia Helfer, 1974) is a divorced mother of two children and a very rich, independent and important lawyer.

The male characters on the other hand are either "free" from any responsibility, not committing to any relationship, no girlfriend, children or bonds of any kind. They enjoy parties, women and materialistic satisfaction, like Lucifer.

Others are the complete opposite, sweet, calm and caring but with lack of initiative as Daniel, Chloe's ex husband (Kevin Alejandro, 1976). He prefers waiting and giving space without rushing things. He doesn't want to put pressure on anybody and is very concerned about the other people's feelings.

All characters doubt and question themselves from time to time and there is no hierarchy, nobody tells the other what to do or even to change (except of the devil's mother of course, go figure!) Everybody is trying to understand the other, but remains independent and there's not even competition among them. Everybody makes their own choices after introspection. Even the angel Amenadiel (D.B. Woodside 1969) is doubting himself, his life choices and the difference between right and wrong. No self-absorbed, know- it-all. He often talks to his brother Lucifer about his thoughts and decisions and keeps an open mind for other ideas or perspectives.

Lucifer is a perfect GenXer: The devil, a fallen angel who has led a rebellion against his father (God) and as a punishment was sent to hell. But after a long time he fled and went to earth, disobeying his father's orders, just doing what he wants and not living by his father's rules anymore. He doesn't want to be what others expect from him but only himself. Sick of being manipulated he tries to do what *he* desires, opposing himself to the life and the role that was chosen for him by his father. Does that ring a bell?

Also "The Good place" talks about heaven and hell but in a very different manner. Here we see a GenXer woman (Kirsten Bell, 1980) in her afterlife, meeting a Baby Boomer "chief" (Ten Danson 1947) and some Millennials that have died with her. (Jameela Jamil 1986), Manuel Jacinto (1987) and William Harper (1980). You can see that the approach towards dealing with problems and challenges are completely different between the generations. I don't want to get too much into the story or spoil anything. But our main character is the one thinking outside the box. Millennials all put themselves in the center, questioning if *their* behavior or *their* attitude towards life could change anything. Whereas the main character observes what happens behind the scenes and finds new and creative ways to find their way out of trouble.

"The After Life" (with Ricky Gervais) is a hilarious dark comedy about an ordinary man who is deeply struck by the death of his wife. He doesn't even try to hide his grief even if he makes others uncomfortable. He is mostly calm and silent in his pain but when other people try to cheer him up he reacts brilliantly cynical and gratuitously offensive.

His remarks are so specific and true that he leaves the counterpart speechless. He just wants to be left alone in his sorrow and wants to make clear that nothing can make him feel better or will ease his pain. So when people try to cheer him up or try to make him feel better he responds in a few words so directly and explicitly that they immediately back off and leave him alone. He knows the dark place in his soul that makes him bitter and cynical because nothing will make his pain go away. He wants to be accepted as he is: sad and grieving and not pretending to be happy.

He is showing his dark side, even though many people don't want to see or accept it. But *we* know that it is part of life, the light and the dark - we all have both sides within us.

He shows his dark side to the world and only few people can accept him in this state. Just like "Lucifer" and "The Good Place", both show us that we all have a bright and a dark side within us. They are not good or bad. They are just parts of our soul.

We GenXers have embraced our dark side and are sick of showing only the "happy" and "perfect" part that society would like to see. We have both parts within us and the world should accept us and also the others without judging.

This is why "The After Life" is so deliberating: it openly says the incredible honest truth. Not all Good is Good or Evil only Evil.

Our dark side is a part of us and we GenXers are OK with that. We just cannot tell anyone, especially Baby Boomers. They will do all in their power to make your dark side go away, expel the bad, destroy and eradicate it. Only one winner, only the light.

Others think that dark is evil or weak and must be hidden or masqueraded. But we know the truth, it won't work and its not necessary.

If we can accept us as a whole, we are free.

9. NEVER MIND

We grew up in a self-centered and self-entitled society. In a world that was too busy to listen to their kids. Adults were more interested in politics, their careers and self-realization. Nobody would ask us what we really wanted. Our parents and teachers knew it all better, so when it came to choices, our opinion was not taken in consideration too much.

If we tried to object, we had to face a "get over it" or worse, endless discussions or better *monologues*. We had to listen why *they* where right and *we* were wrong until we finally agreed to what they said, just to get it over with.

If we had been victim of injustice at home or in school, well, that's the way it was. Mostly the answer was: *"don't make it a drama"* and *"what doesn't kill you will only make you stronger"* or *"there's nothing I can do about it, so stop whining"*.

And which small crying GenXer kid doesn't remember the fantastic sentence: *"I will give you something to cry about"?* Completely different from today, where parents defend they children no matter what, even if they are wrong. Growing up with no defense made us realize two things:

1. everybody is on their own, we cannot rely on anybody
2. "let's talk it out" means that somebody explains to you in an endless monologue why they are right and you are wrong, it's *not* a dialogue and nobody wants to hear your side of the story.

Both mean the same thing: Nobody cares for what you think so keep it to yourself. That's what the Baby Boomers and Silent Generation (grandparents and teachers) taught us.

It's not like we've never tried to speak up our minds, oh no. We have done so. In many occasions. And we've been either laughed at or punished for it. In school any other idea but the teachers' got crushed and each time we tried to speak our mind or to disagree with our teachers or parents we had to pay for it. Big times. Physical punishment was not legal anymore but they had their own methods to make us pay. So we have decided collectively to shut down.

We just didn't *argue* anymore, we just *did* what we wanted. Without any discussion. We don't need to talk to anybody to make up our minds, we know exactly who we are and what we want. And what we *don't* want. We don't need anybody to approve our ideas or tell us if we are right or wrong. We just have our *own* idea and that's enough. We really don't care what others think about us. They don't even bother to know the truth.

"Who cares?" was one of our go-to phrases.

The answer was always *nobody*.

This is why GenXers don't like talking to much. It's superfluous in many cases. We didn't experience conversation as a mutual discussion and in many cases that hasn't changed until today when we try talk to Boomers or Millennials. There's hardly any dialogue, so we prefer walking away just to save the energy. It's just not worth it. Most of the time they are so convinced and self-absorbed that they don't even notice that we are not talking. We prefer to wait and observe. Try to figure out things on our own. And we are very very good at it.

Even today we live in a gray zone where nobody *sees* us. Even on "SNL" (Saturday Night Live on NBC since 1975) there are parodies of Baby Boomers vs Millennials, clearly impersonated by GenXers, but nobody besides *us* even noticed that.

Everybody is so concentrated on what they see about *their* generation, that they completely miss out on the whole parody of GenXers playing both parts. When they asked one of the characters played by Kenan Thompson he joked "I am Gen X, I just sit on the sidelines and watch the world burn".

That sums it up. We are an independent and self sufficient generation and we just don't get it why people are so narcissistic and self absorbed that they need the spotlight all the time. SNL is great by the way, very cynical and realistic as most GenXers love it. We just watch the two generations fight and they don't even notice that we exist as well.

Very entertaining.

In the early 90s when child raising morphed from "get over it" to "praise your child everyday" things turned around.

Suddenly kids were asked, what their point of view was, they were told to speak up without being punished for a different opinion and praised for just everything. Before that, only winners got a medal, but now everybody got a "participation trophy".

It was ridiculous. For us yet again that was just another craziness. Until some years earlier we were basically told to shut up all the time and now they wanted to speak to us, know what was on our minds? No, we didn't fall for that anymore. Even teachers tried to ask us what we thought about some topics for a brief moment but than went straight back to teaching what *they* thought was right.

Do you know what nowadays Gen Z (and also Millennials) reply to a question they don't want to answer? *"Whatever"*. Interesting. So you basically tell the counterpart that they are right, just like a "whatever you want" - just stop arguing.

We didn't say "whatever" we said something very different:

Never mind

It doesn't mean choose whatever you want.

It means don't even *bother* to ask me.

Don't waste your energy.

You don't really want to know anyway.

10. MUSIC

In the 1970s and 1980s we witnessed some new music trends and lots of really cool Rock and Pop Ions. From Jimi Hendrix and Woodstock over to the Queen, U2, and to pop with ABBA, Michael Jackson, and Madonna, you name it.

Every week a new fabulous album was released and we loved to listen to the soundtracks of some movies that were about as famous as the movies themselves (Hair, Dirty Dancing, Top Gun etc).

When we became teenagers many of us had their own little rock bands and we tried to make some music in somebody's garage. The only problem was pretty obvious. Whatever we tried to play, our parents had already done it *better.*

They had Woodstock, Live Aid 85, all the best bands and music. How can you try to be creative when whatever you do it just smiled at from above with a downplaying comment like "but *our* music is so much better, your generation doesn't know how to make music". That's what all generations say, but for us is was really difficult. Our parent's music was "disgusting" to *their* parents, so they would crank up the volume even more. But they didn't hate ours like their parents had hated theirs. They liked rock. But theirs was *better.*

More rebellious, louder, meaner, more meaningful. Better lyrics. Against war in Vietnam, social problems. Ours in comparison was ridiculous.

Some new bands came up but they always remained somehow it the shadow, making really good music, but still *rock* music, nothing new. But we wanted something on our own, as every generation, we needed our own genre to express what we felt.

In the 70s music and clothes were very loud and flashy to the excessive with weird color patterns and big collars, very eccentric and sexy.

That changed in the 1980s. Now everything became "neat" and polished. All perfect and presentable. Music was aired on TV and the bands had changed their image. Mostly in playback and the lighting and make up was impeccable. In TV everything had to be perfect, everybody styled with perfect hair and so as kids we didn't experience music in concerts but in TV as the polished, perfect, studio version of the "idea" of the band.

Most GenXers grew up watching MTV and we couldn't wait for a new album being released. We knew every video by heart and were completely absorbed by music. It was everywhere, on the radio, in movies and of course on MTV.

We followed our favorite bands and stars and tried to catch every interview, every small glimpse behind the scenes of a new video and hung up posters of our favorite bands in our room. We grew up with TV and also the music that we were listening to, often was introduced to us by MTV, the "Music Television" Channel launched in 1981.

In the beginning it was entirely about music, in Europe only one station aired in English for the entire audience. There were different shows for every category: "Headbanger's ball" was exclusively about heavy metal, on "MTV unplugged" the bands performed with acoustic instruments and "Yo-Raps" introduced us to the latest of Hip Hop. We kept MTV in the background like a Radio to listen to our favorite songs.

On "MTV most wanted" we could send a handwritten letter (!) to a mailbox and days later we would see the desired video on the show. I had written a letter a week earlier to my 18th birthday, leaving also my phone number (landline of course, there were no cell phones yet, silly!). Surprisingly the TV host 'Ray Cokes' actually called when I was home with my friends to wish me a happy birthday and asked me for my favorite song! I have to admit it, I chose "keep the faith" by Jon Bon Jovi that day, my friends were thrilled!

MTV also called back 10 minutes later to make me participate in the "Goody-bag-competition" where one could win gadgets. I won an original MTV T-shirt and still keep it as a relic. It's priceless.

We always saw the release of a new song on MTV, we knew all the shows and news about the bands. That's why we are also called

The "*MTV Generation*".

In 1993 MTV introduced "Beavis and Butthead", an adult animated satire, full of quotes and critical commentary on society. We loved their cynical, stupid and crazy adventures.

While we were watching MTV, our parents generation had converted from Hippies to Yuppies, the economy was doing good in the Western world and everybody liked to show off their wealth.

Perfect families on TV, sad things were hidden and everybody was supposed to be happy and perfect. "Don't worry, be happy" was the slogan by Bobby McFerrin in 1988 and the "Smiley" was printed on stickers, T-shirts and magazines.

At the end of the 1980s we were so sick of it. Now we just needed a new music style on our own, to finally show the Boomers that also we, Gen X, created some really good music. Then, finally, what had started in the mid 80s as the "Seattle Sound" became the first symbol of a generation and grew to its full potential with Nirvana and Pearl Jam in the 1990s: *GRUNGE*.

Finally putting away the fake happy side and allowing for us to show our frustration and the darkness inside. We finally had our own music and a *name* to represent it. In the early 1990s the first pure Gen X bands emerged, revolutionizing music and creating new music styles like Rap, Metal, Brit pop, independent rock and cross overs, like:

"the Smashing Pumpkins" with Billy Corgan (1967), D'arcy Wretzky (1968), Jamles Iha (1968) and Jimmy Chamberlin (1964)

"Oasis" Liam Gallager (1972), Noel Gallager (1967),

Paul Arthurs "Bonehead" (1965) and Paul Mc Guigan (1971).

"Green Day" Billie Joe (1972), Trè Cool (1972), Mike Dirnt (1972), Al Sobrante (1969) and Blake Ronnie (1972) and countless other bands like:

"Rage against the machine" by Zack de la Roche (1970), Tom Morelo (1964), Tim Crommerford (1968) and Brad Wilk (1968) who translated all our rage and frustration into words and music.

Rock festivals were organized everywhere and we went to lots of them, even if obviously our parents had been to "much better" festivals (Woodstock) with "better" bands and "better" music. Of course.

Most Baby Boomers had never been to festivals at all, but they collectively "experienced" Woodstock as if it was something they had actually attended, so any other festival could never compete in their eyes. But we didn't care, it was finally OUR time, OUR music and OUR moment.

We went to Rock Festivals to listen to Green Day, The Offspring, Counting Crows, Bad Religion, Guns 'n Roses, Soundgarden, The Red Hot Chilly Peppers, Radio Head, Blur, Garbage, Manic Street Preachers, Biohazard, Skunk Anansie and so many more.. but above all.. Pearl Jam.

The difference to our parent's generation was, that our bands were *not* free to express themselves. All our CDs had the white sticker on the cover claiming *"parental advisory-explicit lyrics"* and some parents wouldn't allow their teenage children to buy those CDs. Now that was contradictory.

Baby Boomers had listened to the most explicit Rock n' Roll lyrics on earth with singers doing crazy things on stage that were unimaginable (try to google Ozzy Osbourne and Frank Zappa)...but when *our* generation tried to express itself, we were judged, labeled and *banned*..

Still trying to judge and constrain our music, some lyrics or entire videos were banned from MTV and many had to create a "clean" version of the song if they wanted to be published. Can you imagine the music of the 70s in a "clean version"? "parental advisory" stickers would have had to be everywhere.

But no, the Generation before us was allowed to listen to songs against war, talking about killing and rebellion, but not *us*. We were controlled, cut in power and expression. Also the video "Zombie" by the Cranberries was initially banned from BBC. *Freedom of expression* was not applicable to the new generation. What was their name again?

X...whatever. Slackers!

But also our generation loved to hang out at festivals where one could try bungee jumping for the first time (see X-treme sports), have a piercing or get a tattoo. That, too, was *our* thing, whereas for the previous generations tattoos were only for prisoners or Vietnam-war-veterans, we just had them for fun. Also piercing became very popular among GenXers although many had serious problems at home, at school and work for being "different".

We were denied jobs, bullied and some parents didn't talk to their own kids anymore after they had gotten a piercing or tattoo. One was immediately judged a "criminal" .

Today Millennials and Gen Z think that it's *their* achievement. You have no idea what the first GenXers went through to make tattoos socially accepted. Today even teenagers get a "sleeve" and everybody can have tattoos on their hands, neck and arms and it's no big deal anymore. So you Millennials think it's your thing? Well, I'm sorry, it isn't. If you can get a tattoo nowadays without any repercussion, it's also thanks to us. *You're welcome.*

Going back to the festivals with independent and rock music where we had our own vibe, expressing our anger and frustration. Being anything but polished and neat, here's where the tattoos and piercings fit in, perfectly. After our years of rebellion in the 1990s (like our parents in the 1970s) we changed in the years to come, even if lots of us still love rock music and play in their own bands.

The rebellion went on, but after letting our frustration and rage out for years, we wanted to pass on to something more fun. In the early 2000 Hip Hop and Bling Style made everybody party and we didn't care for clean versions or politically correctness, it was all the opposite, very straight forward and just inviting to party and having a good time.

11. THE COOL GENERATION

We loved the directness, the energy and the vibe of RAP, HIP HOP and R&B, cynical and powerful. Snoop Dogg (1971), Tupac (1971), Ice Cube (1969), The Game (1979), 50 Cent (1975), Akon (1973), Eminem (1972) and the notorious BIG (1972) just to name a few, are all GenXers and personified perfectly the Hip Hop vibe in the 00's.

Just partying, having fun no matter what, despite the anger ,hate and frustration, just get over it, name the things by their name, describe things the way they are, and just party. That's a feeling that we embraced to the fullest. Party no matter what, put everything aside and just have fun.

That's why *we* are the *"cool"* generation. We have been through it, we know that there is pain and anger in life but we know that somethings can't be changed. So why not let it go and move on? You can call us *anything*, we are used to that. We remain calm in any situation, we are patient.

That's why we are thoroughly *cool*. Nobody can beat us. We hardly ever get upset. We can wait it out. Resilient survivors, remember? We care too little. They called us "disaffected" and "apathetic". We just expect the worst to happen. We've *lost our illusion...*

If you say anything to a Baby Boomer they get *immediately* defensive, angry and usually very loud. Many Millennials on the other side are short of patience and get straight upset and want everything right now.

GenXers are the really cool ones. Other Generations hate us for that. LOL. They think that we don't care. Well, maybe that's true. We just don't. You think what you want to think and I keep my opinion anyway. I don't have to "win". That's why we stay "cool" in an argument. And that makes the others go crazy, if we just say nothing.

No need to argue.

Our power lies in our patience.

And besides that, have you seen a GenXer doing extreme sports? There's nothing cooler than that. Not because we are still doing it in our forties and fifties, but because we *sincerely* don't care what anybody thinks about us.

We just go ahead and do it. You think what you want to think, you say what you want to say, that doesn't affect us. We just do it for fun, for ourselves. If you don't like it that's your problem, not ours. We are not harming anybody, so mind your own business and let go. From this day forward I would like to refer to Generation X as

"the Cool Generation".

Because we literally *are* the *cool* generation.

(smiley face with sunglasses)...

and that's something to be proud of!

12. THE INTERNET

Talking about inventions and the internet, guess what is another completely overlooked creation by GenXers used everyday by millions of people worldwide? Small hint: it's for free.

Every time you want to know something about anything, a country, a person, a fact...what is your first move?

You take your smart phone and.. exactly, "Google" it. It has become so much part of our lives that many think it has been here forever, like the earth, the moon and the sky. "To google" has even become a verb and many don't even do *anything* (buy a product, go out on a date or hire somebody) without first "google" them.

Wow. Google. Really? For new Generations it is part of their lives, like the internet or smartphones. But it has not always been around. Google was founded only in 1998 by two GenXers: Larry Page, 1973 and Sergey Brin 1973 and is now the most used web based search engine worldwide.

Try to google that! Fun fact, when I tried to do some research for this book I tried to find some information about Gen X. There is hardly any at all. I found very few videos about Generation X, almost all of them produced Millennials. They talk mainly about Baby Boomers and obviously themselves but the few things they said about Gen X were plain wrong.

Like that Gen X had to "adapt" to the internet. It's actually the other way around: GenXers have *invented* most of the services that many people base their daily lives on today. Try to imagine one day without Google, YouTube and Wikipedia, where do you get your information from?

But GenXers don't brag about it, hardly anybody knows their names and the best part of it is, that all of these services are free. Not like all the things that *we* had to *pay* for growing up, like music and films. Now you can find them on YouTube. It has been given to the user for free, there's no "annual subscription" or a membership to pay for. Of course they earn money from the sponsors but for the end user, it's for free.

All you "have" to do is watch an Ad now and then (what a burden, uh?) and people today get crazy about that. Hey, it's for free, what do you expect? I know that the new generations pretend everything for free as if it was their birth-right but there are people who have decided deliberately to give it out for free as a gift and take the money from the Ads. Think about that for a minute.

Without Google, Wikipedia and YouTube you would be back in the 1980s and 1990 when we grew up. Or anytime prior to that of course when dinosaurs ruled the earth. Yawn.

It just took us forever to get any information. If we were lucky our parents had a 24-pieces encyclopedia ad home, a shelf full of big, heavy and expensive books from A to Z. It was our only source of information before Google. Let's say somebody told us that "Quokkas" were funny or we had heard about them on the radio or in a movie. So we took the big, heavy and dusty book from the shelf, displaying a giant, golden "Q" on the front cover and started flipping through the thin pages.

If we didn't know how it was spelled correctly, there was no "auto-correction" so we maybe tried to look up "Cocca" first and never found it it the "C" book. What a waste of time. There was no intelligent search machine telling us "maybe you're looking for "Quokka". Aha. That would have been awesome.

So much for patience. It took a lot of effort to look up something, so we needed lots and lots of it. If we hadn't been patient we would have never learned anything.

I guess that new generations, who rely on "Google" for information, would go crazy trying to search an item in an encyclopedia. Would be an interesting sociological experience.

So back in the days when we finally found the word we were looking for, like "Quokka", it just said: "Quokka, pouched mammal, living in Australia". No pictures, no videos, no other info whatsoever.

So much for disillusion. See? All the pieces of the puzzle are falling into place.

If we wanted to know more we had to go to an actual library or bookshop and try to find a book about animals in Australia. Maybe the book would have some pictures or more enlightenment on that topic, if we were lucky that was our next birthday gift. Today with Google we can have pictures, videos on You Tube and a very exhaustive explanation by a Quokka expert on Wikipedia in seconds without even getting up from the couch. Maybe even our favorite celebrity taking selfies with one. By the way, Quokkas seem to smile and love to take selfies! I am pretty sure that almost everybody is googling "Quokka" at this point.

This is all possible thanks to GenXers, giving us all these services for free. Don't take it for granted. Just for once, stop and be thankful for what this generation has given to you. It has not been like that before, we had to spend a lot of time, energy and money to get all these services. Search for explications, buy books or pay for lessons. Today, if we want the lyrics to a song we just type the title + "lyrics" on YouTube and somebody has done the work for you. On Spotify and YouTube people create playlists for free so we can listen to all the music that reflect our taste and preferences without the fatigue of gathering the songs together.

Our approach to the internet started right away with the invention of the same. We grew up playing video games at home as kids, first on TV and then on the computer, we are the first generation growing up with digital technology.

We used to play video games on Atari and Commodore Amiga consoles. The games consisted in blocks and points moving around, a lot of imagination and patience was required to even get into the games. The programs themselves were still very basic so there were no colored icons but just a black screen with amber or green letters and numbers. Executing even simple commands or copying a "floppy disk" (a removable, external memory "card" with roughly1 MB of capacity) was a little tricky and at least basic programming skills and understanding were required to operate them.

In 1985 the first "Microsoft Windows" Operating system was released and later with "Windows 93" and "Windows 95" everybody could use a computer. There was a digital desktop with icons on the screen, just like today, and we just had to drag the icons around to achieve the desired action. From that moment on even people with no technical expertise could use computers and the personal computer was brought into almost every home.

At the same time internet was becoming more and more popular, because more people had a computer to connect to the internet. Of course the first modems were all attached to the landline of our phones and while somebody was online the phone couldn't be used. No WiFi or smartphones yet, of course. We are the Generation that grew up together with the technology, we slowly gained more and more informatics skills and witnessed the changes from analogue to digital. We can work with both because we have actually used both in our lives.

We went from Cassettes, Tape Decks and LPs over CD players and basic Computers to i-Pods and now smart phones. We use digital and analog, with the greatest of ease.

We know *how* and *why* both work and where they came from, we have seen the history and the evolution of the digital world. We went from wall-attached telephones with a dialing disk, over to wireless, then cellphones and later to smartphones. And we have used them along the way. We didn't *adapt* to anything, we *grew up* together. Floppy disk or CD, SD cards or USB sticks, recording a tape while listening to the radio or making a new playlist for our car on an USB stick, we can handle all of these technologies. We are very creative and use our patience and skills to understand the next level and evolve with it.

Many of the top used Services on the Internet were invented by GenXers:

"Google": Sergey Brin (1973) and Larry Page (1973)

"YouTube": Jawed Karim (1979), Steve Chen (1978) and Chad Hurley (1977)

"Twitter": Jack Dorsay (1976), Evan Williams (1972), Biz Stone (1974) and Noah Glass (1981)

"Napster": founded by Shawn Fenning (1980) and Sean Parker (1979), was launched and closed down many times.

"WhatsApp": founded by Jan Koum (1976) and Brian Acton (1972) and later sold to the "Face Book"- Group.

Gen X business model was basically anarchy. We didn't want to follow Baby Boomers business model based on

"inventing something and squeeze all the money out of the customer for using it. Don't give anything for free if you can make some profit."

We were fed up with old business models of using new technology to enslave people, like buying a new TV, paying for cable, getting a new computer and making the user pay for every minute online. Gen X didn't want to go on with that idea but the companies that actually developed physical *products* were (and many are still) owned and controlled by Baby Boomers. So our generation first expanded in a world that was new to everybody: the internet We broke the rules because we didn't care about the rules. We made up our *own* rules. Invent something and put it on the internet for free. Like Pirates, the first sites making music and lyrics available for free had been sued and shut down many times.

But GenXers didn't give up. We are very resilient and patient. We try again and again. No big riots in the streets, no burning cars, no chanting protest songs on the street.

GenXers revolutionized all our lives by changing the *internet*, changing the way of perceiving possession. We are the creative ones who think outside the box. We always had to rely on our own patience and creativity.

Just like the ramps we had built for our bikes as kids, if something didn't work out, *we* had to improve it to make it work the next time. No help from outside, no mentors or tutor. Just us. And that's what we took to our advantage.

We wanted to create a better world, we were used to share our value information with our friends (like the lyrics and chords of a song) and we wanted to share them with the world. For free. Make the sponsors pay for it, the ones who then earn from selling their products.

Not the user for using Google, YouTube, Wikipedia or Twitter. That itself was a revolution. The world is so much different now than it was 30 years ago. We share information, images and songs for *free*.

Gen Xers took it from the producers and gave it our to the users. Before "WhatsApp" was introduced in 2009, we had to send images as "*MMS*". 1 dollar each image. We could only call on landline which was very expensive (especially if you wanted to call abroad). Everything was so complicated and pricy. Now it's for free and available everywhere.

That was the change we wanted to see in the world and we gave it to the future generations. To all generations. Even to those who still see us as *slackers*.

You still think Generation X has achieved nothing, still believe that we are no good, that we haven't changed anything, have no goals in life? Really?

I am *proud* to belong to this generation.

And even today, the names of many founders remain unknown. Many don't even know who they are or which generation they belong to.

Most people only know Bill Gates (Baby Boomer) and Mark Zuckerberg (Millennial) and automatically assume that the computer was invented by one and all internet services by the other generation.

As you've seen that's not true at all. I hope that this book finally brings the right consideration to the all the creative, determined and brave GenXers who introduced us to these revolutionary, life-changing innovations.

Thank you.

13. COMMUNICATION

Since we mainly grew up by playing by ourselves or watching TV, MTV or action movies, our brain is hard-wired to respond better to images than to words. We are a *visual* generation, we like pictures and videos and we don't even need words to communicate. Of course we read books, but mainly by ourselves which again is a visual stimulation. Lately we even came up with a form of communication that is just perfect for us GenXers.

Have you ever wondered why "WhatsApp" has "Emojis"? Exactly! The round, yellow face is obviously a longer existing image created in the 1960s for an assurance campaign and in the 1980s the "smiley" was everywhere. Also using "emoticons" in text messages to write a smiling face like so " :) " has been used already in the late 1970s.

So I'm not claiming the smileys to be an Gen X-invention. But we *use* them! On Whats App there is an entire library of items to choose from and we can switch easily from text to emojis, writing a whole concept entirely with tiny, little images. That's perfect for GenXers, we understand each other immediately and need no further explanation. All generations use social media, but everyone is drawn to a different platform and use it in a different manner. On Instagram and Facebook we see GenXers posting pictures of things *they* like or want to *show* to their friends. A place, their pet, a cool instrument or their hobby. I notice that many receive very few "likes"on their posts But that's OK..We don't care too much what others think about us, we want to *share with others* what *we* like.

Millennials instead, mainly post pictures of *themselves*: selfies, pictures with *them* in the foreground or taking up the whole picture, for example *"me* in Paris" and you can see only their face, they could be anywhere. But, of course, they receive lots of "likes".

Many of them pay all the attention to the "likes" they collect. It's not the picture itself what one really "likes" but a proof that one likes the *person* who posted the picture.

Some Millennials crave for attention all the time, they need other people to "like" their posts showing mainly selfies every single day.

We GenXers just don't get it. Yesterday you posted a picture of your face and again today and again tomorrow. What do you want to show me? That you are pretty? OK, I'll give you a "like", you are pretty. But again tomorrow and the day after and again every single day? Come on.. that's so boring.

Is there nothing going on in your life, anything you want to share with us, besides of what you *look* like? Some pictures are so heavily photo-shopped and all available filters applied that you can hardly recognize the person in real life. LOL. I don't see the point, I know you in real life. You don't look like that! Some Millennials have entire profiles with *only* selfies, mainly making a duck face or showing what their bodies look like. You can rarely see them post anything else. Often we can read notes like "I am so tired, I am so old, I am so crazy, I am so lazy"... Notice anything? I am, I am, I am. Me, me, me. Yawn.

That's so boring. And so sad. But I don't blame them. I feel sorry for them, that they need that much attention all the time and the proof that they are important, special and wanted. They grew up with full attention all the time so when you take it away from them they just die like a flower without water. They know that, so they "feed" each others with "likes" all the time.

I consider myself lucky, we GenXers are lucky. We don't have that kind of stress in our lives, that must be exhausting.

Gen Z on the other hand approaches social media in a completely different manner. Many post more of what they are *doing*, instead of portraits of themselves like the Millennials. They also post things they have created and want to share with the world. Many use Snap-chat and TikTok more than Facebook.

We can see them with their friends, following their hobbies and showing what they do in their normal lives. Unboxing parcels, pranking friends or just walking around at home filming their daily life.

They grew up with the internet and are used to watch reality shows, for them "Big Brother" is not a show but rather real life, witnessed by the public. They show songs recorded with their friends and screenshots of conversations between them and others. Their life happens *online*, there is hardly any secret or privacy. They like to have "directs" on

Instagram and show what they eat and drink, watch on TV and say to their friends. Many like to interact, ask questions, make polls and base some of their decisions on what the "public" replies to their questions. Others film themselves gaming and post their last achievements.

Last Year I suffered a car crash with another person and when the police arrived to take notes, they actually asked this question: "Did you take any selfies while you were injured and waiting for the ambulance"?

I was like "what?". Totally confused about the question. It would have never dawned to me to take a selfie in that moment. Anything but that. I had left my whole purse in the car when we fled out of the crashed car to jump the concrete barrier and put ourselves in safety. Only later we got back to the car, retrieved our smartphones and called the ambulance.

I would *never* have thought of taking a selfie in that situation. Apparently now that's what people do and that's why this question is actually part of the current protocol. Wow. Some people are so narcissistic and self absorbed that they need the spotlight all the time.

Even when their life is in danger.

That's incredible.

14. MONEY

Most of us were raised by our Baby Boomers/Silent Generation parents and by our grandparents who most likely were from the Greatest or Silent Generation.

Our grandparents had witnessed the war and especially in Europe they had vivid memories of times of hunger and deprivation. So they raised us not to waste any food, be very careful with our money and treat our things with respect so that they would last for a long time.

We were taught the value of money and that we had to work hard for it. Many of us had some small side business before or after school: babysitting, carrying out newspapers or helping the neighbors to wash their cars or mow the lawn.

We learned that we had to do a good job, otherwise they would make us do it again until it was right. No excuses allowed. If we wanted a bigger present we had to wait for Christmas or our birthday and so we had to practice a lot of patience.

In the 1990s most GenXers joined the workforce, and we were ready to work hard for our money. Also there we had to be very patient. Most of us started with an internship, hardly payed anything or nothing at all, we were supposed to be happy to work for free and to get an idea of what the real world would be like.

So we did our best to see and to learn as much as we could so that maybe one day we would get a decent payed job like our parents.

But there was a much bigger thing going on a global scale. The economic boom couldn't last forever. The Gross Domestic product (GDP) in the US started to low down in the 1960s. From the mid 1970s and afterwards the US debt began to increase faster than the GDP. The public debt reached a post war low of 24.6% in 1974. In that year the congressional budget and impoundment control act of 1974 reformed the budget process and Ronald Reagan lowered the tax rates in the US in the 1980s.

As a result the public dept rose from 26.2% in 1980 to 40.9% in 1988 reaching 48.3% in 1992. That meant that taxes got higher, prices went up and the inflation started to rise. We already had been told in school that when we would enter the work force we would have had to pay for all the debt that our parents had left us.

Very discouraging: we were told to go to school, study, then find a job and to pay of *their* debt in taxes. Our parent's lifestyle with low taxes and plenty of opportunities wasn't payed by *themselves*. They decided to make *us* and the later generations pay for it all when we were still kids.

Then, in January 1999 when most of the GenXers had just started to get a small Job, the European Union introduced the EURO. The idea was to have one currency in most European countries. The idea wasn't too bad, but the reality was quite a bummer. Bearing in mind that 1 Euro was about 2 German Marks (1,955 DM), 2000 Italian Lira's (1936 ITL), about 2 Dutch Guilder (2,203 NLG) and so on.

With the Euro all wages were basically cut in *half*, instead of a monthly income of 2000 DM after taxes, one would earn 1000 Euro. (The Millennials are called "Generation 1000 Euro" in Spain for a reason).

So 48.000 DM annually were converted into 24.000 (before taxes) in Euro.

So far so good. The prices were supposed to be cut in half, too. Instead of paying 1 DM for a Coffee it was supposed to be 50 Euro-cents.

But that wasn't the case. Not even one year later all the prices had basically doubled. A coffee didn't cost 50 cents but 1 Euro, the rent for a small apartment doubled from 700 DM straight to 700 Euros, with now the wages being cut in half.

So our purchase power was cut in half within a single year. We had always been told that we were supposed to join the workforce to pay off our parents debts but this was too much. Also the small amount of money that we had in the bank and that we had been making sacrifices for, was cut in half.

Today we have to work exactly *twice* as much to earn the *same* money. That's why only one parent working had never been an option for us.

All our dreams of one day living a decent life with a stable job had been shattered. Only 2 years later, in 2001 the world was changed again by 9/11.

The US debt had doubled from 2000 to 2008, from 5,674,178,209,886,86 USD to 10,024724896,912,75 USD (source: treasury direct). War expenses skyrocketed and taxes rose. People were forced to borrow money and with higher prices and less money struggled to pay of mortgages and loans. Property prices started to fall and lead to a collapse of the assets.

In 2007-2008 the global financial crisis was the worst economic disaster after the great depression. Yet again our grandparents had been right. You'll never know what will happen tomorrow. And yet again, we had to get trough it. Some went to live abroad, some started their own business, most just work hard and carry on, knowing that our parents will be also the last generation to enjoy a retirement, if so. We have to rely on 401(K). We know that we are *doomed*.

According to a study by the "Experian" in April 17th 2019, GenXers have more debt than all the other generations. The average counts 125,000 USD vs Baby Boomers with 88,313 and Millennials with 52,120 USD. They don't only take care of their children but also their parents, shouldering more financial responsibilities than the others. When you hear people say "In my days everything was better" that's most probably a Baby Boomer. Yes, for **them** it *was* better. Low taxes and easy loans, a son of a farmer could become a lawyer.

Our grandparents from silent generation or the greatest generation have never said *anything* like that. All they said was "You're lucky you have to eat, lots of nice things and all those toys" and "In my days it was hard.". I have *never* heard them say "it was better in the old days".

15. NUTRITION

Ironically the greatest and silent generation had little to eat after the war, but the food they had was genuine. Whole food, no OGM, no food colors, no artificial added chemicals, just the plain thing.

Lots of them lived up to a very old age, many achieved 90 and some even 100 years. With the economic boom in the 1950s and 1960s, when the Baby Boomers grew up, there was more to eat and their parents had the idea that 'a fat baby was a healthy baby', so they stuffed them with lots of food and made sure that they always ate enough or even too much.

After WWII the economy boomed in the occidental world because consumerism was highly influenced and promoted by advertisements and campaigns. The idea that 'animal products were the best for your offspring' was claimed by the media to push the consumption.

Children had to drink lots of milk and eat lots of meat every day to become 'strong and healthy'. Sugar was added to everything and there was lots of misinformation about what was healthy. Even smoke was supposed to be good for loosing weight and doctor's advice was pretty much the contrary of what it is today when it comes to nutrition standards.

In the US the government issued a guideline of the food pyramid, which suggested to eat a lot of carbs, with bread and flower-based foods, adding some veggies, meat and some sweets. The economic boom made people in the occidental world think that they had to make up for all the deprivation they had endured during war, so the "wealth belly" was shown with pride, because a fat family could afford lots of food.

Some people sat outside on their bench after lunchtime with a toothpick in their mouth to make the neighbors believe that they were rich and could afford meat.

The interesting fact here is that grandmothers from the silent generation made (and those alive still *make*) their children and grandchildren eat lots of heavy and high caloric food. As if we still had to gain weight to make it through winter or had to work twelve hours in the fields. But if you observe them closer *they* themselves don't eat all that food.

It' s only for the children and their offspring which they love to stuff with lots of incredible heavy food to show their affection.

Members of the silent generation are often very long-living or when they get sick it's mostly in their 80s or 90s. Baby Boomers instead had a very different experience. Due to the high animal protein and sugar loaded diet combined with heavy smoking and a sedentary lifestyle, many suffered from cardio vascular diseases, diabetes, strokes or cancer already in their 50s and 60s. Many baby Boomers don't practice sport or have an active lifestyle. Few do some soft gymnastics but mostly it's not enough to built some muscle to protect their bones or their heart and lungs.

When I ask GenXers what they ate as kids many have to laugh. There was nothing healthy, wholegrain or even gluten-free or without lactose in their diet. We GenXers grew up in a time when kids were fed the worst food imaginable. In the 1970s and 1980s it was all carbs, sugar, food colorants, the invention of processed food of any kind and microwave dinners.

We drank soft drinks and had white bread with no nutritional value, sweet bread-spreads squeezed out of a tube and anything that was quick and easy for our parents to prepare. No more long hours in the kitchen like our grandmas but instant soups and sauces, instant food just to pop in the microwave and .. voilà! dinner was ready.

Many women joined the work force and others had found themselves a hobby so they didn't have the time or wanted to stay all day in the kitchen to prepare food, as their mothers had done. So the food industry came up with solutions.

The advertisement told us that a processed bar was a healthy breakfast and that sugar was important for our well-being. Animal products and diary was still supposed to be good for us and were consumed at least 3 times a day.

Wheat had been genetically modified in the 1970s and became lower in protein and higher in carbs. That's why gluten was already a problem in the 1970s and 1980s but if we were intolerant, we just had no idea why we were always sick and had to 'suck it up'. *"Bread and milk is good for you, stop whining!"*

There were always the "poor kids in Africa" that had nothing to eat, thanks to "live Aid 1985". The concert organized by Bob Geldof and Midge Ure to raise funds for the famine in Ethiopia showed us life pictures of children starving to death. So we were supposed to be happy for what we had and shut up. *"Spoiled brats"*.

But that didn't help children suffering from intolerance to gluten or dairy. Our complaints or concerns found deaf ears. *"We eat whats on the table"*. End of story.

Today I see kids drinking water and have their food customized to their needs, lactose-free, gluten-free sugar-free and so on. We had nothing free, soft drinks came in neon colors and even gummy bears were all in different, vivid colors. Today they basically are all white.

Our food had all kind of chemical based ingredients, flavor enhancers and conservators. We were fed sugars, colorants, wheat and diary despite of any allergy or problems. Advertisements showed how funny, easy and quick our food was to prepare. Astronauts promoted colored soft-drinks and athletes claimed to eat sweets that gave them energy.

Cigarettes and alcohol were promoted on TV as the coolest, relaxing, adventurous thing for adults to do.

Food wasn't supposed to be healthy but quick, cheap and easy to prepare, so that it often remained the only food choice available.

16. FOOD CHIOCES

Luckily most of made different food choices as adults. In the 1990s I decided to become vegetarian which in that time was extremely difficult. Today people can become easily vegan but the 1990s trying to find anything without meat or fish was almost impossible.

There was no meat substitute in supermarkets and the only choice was to eat more veggies, eggs and cheese and sometimes tofu found in ethnic shops. Restaurants had almost no dish at all without meat or fish and in the end often I was presented a dish with ham. The explanation was always: "but it's not meat, just ham". Often I just ate *nothing* but bread sticks and went back home hungry.

What some of us had started as a healthy diet, later on became a lifestyle. I hoped to reduce my carbon footprint and animal suffering by consuming as little animal products as possible. In the last 30 years that has gotten easier luckily, because more and more people demand for a healthier diet and better food options.

Today in most places you can find something healthy or designed to meet your needs at least in the supermarkets. In restaurants this is still often very problematic and you have to have lots of patience and persistence to get something to eat at all that is either vegan, vegetarian without gluten or dairy.

Many GenXers have chosen their own diet whereas most Baby Boomers never changed and stick to what they ate when they were kids. Many still consume way to much sugar, salt, fats and white flours. For the Baby Boomers that *was* and still *is* the right way to eat. Many suffer from diabetes and cardiovascular diseases, but even though, they prefer taking pills and keep on having the same diet rather that changing their way of eating.

Most GenXers instead are trying to eat healthier than what they were fed when they were young. We know that processed and greasy food leads to disease and makes us feel miserable. Also here the self-doubt and the self-reflection comes into place: whereas Baby Boomers continue with the same habits throughout their lives, never questioning if any of this might harm them, the environment or anybody else, GenXers have a different approach.

We don't only reflect about our behavior but also our way of consuming and inevitably about our way of eating. The consequences for our health, the planet or the environment.

Becoming adults who work in the food industry, many GenXers have invented better food options, making good food choices available to everybody.

Many grannies from the silent generation still cook very heavily for their children and grandchildren but eat very few themselves. Lots of them hardly consume any meat products, processed or greasy foods at all, they just make everyone else do that. Curious fact: I know many grandmothers that cook for everybody but when you ask them to join you at the table, they always have some excuse, they are busy cooking, want to leave the best to you or don't like to eat much in the first place.

Today in many countries you can find food for all specific needs even if the struggle is not over yet. But whether somebody tries to find biologically grown or no OGM food, vegan, gluten- or lactose -free at least nowadays it is mandatory to list all the ingredients and the nutritional value on the package. To leave the choice to the final consumer.

We can also look up products on Wikipedia, YouTube and Google, so our choices can be based on something real. Nobody can argue anymore with the fact that they don't know that some foods have lots of calories because it is printed right there on the package.

Nobody can claim that they don't know that tobacco can cause serious problems or death. One has do *decide* to ignore the facts. Today all the ingredients and the making of a product are not only listed on the package itself but there are some great videos and advice by doctors, personal trainers and nutrition specialists that can answer any questions.

They can give lots of options on how to fuel one's body properly. Once it was a trial and error and without nutritional value it was hard to find out, if and what, one was intolerant or allergic to. Now we know that by avoiding gluten or dairy some people can resolve many of their health problems.

Of course every day there are new discoveries and some people are into either one diet or another but it is impossible to argue that one cannot eat healthy because they don't have a clue which products are healthy and which aren't.

Most GenXers are also more into sports than Baby Boomers and we can only hope that this, combined with a healthy diet, will make up for the poor food choices that we had as kids.

17. GENDER ROLES

Our grandmothers during the war, were often left alone and had to take care of everything, while their husbands were far away somewhere in the battle. Some remained widows for all their lives, others went back to the traditional life style when their husbands came home.

In the 1970s there was a revolution of women gaining more power, they could decide whether or not to have children, to divorce or be independent. Feminism was discussed publicly and the new world was supposed to give equal chances to boys and girls.

So we, the GenXers were the *first* generation to grow up with that new concept. We grew up with the idea that a woman not only *could* be strong and *could* do everything, but basically *had to be* strong *and* do everything.

We were *told* what were supposed to be doing but had no role model. I'm not saying that independence is a bad thing and I am absolutely not talking about women's rights, these of course are absolutely necessary in a modern society and as we all know that equal treatment and equal payment are far away from being realized even 30 years later. I am talking about *gender roles* in society. In the 1970s there were heated discussions about if if was OK for the woman to go join the workforce and leave the kids at home or the scandal if somebody got divorced.

The debates were always about them, the *adults*. Never about us kids. We were never asked for what we wanted but had to suck it up and deal with it.

Our Baby Boomer parents disrupted the scheme of old gender roles when they were young adults and taught us to grow up as strong girls from a very young age.

Being "feminine" was synonym for being "weak" and we were supposed to be though. Finally we could do, what our mom's couldn't do as kids, like wearing jeans. But we couldn't really choose either, we were *supposed* to do that. Even to girls they said "don't be such a girl" as if that was a bad thing to be.

The idea of a *good* woman was a *strong* woman that behaved like a man, but still looked seductive to men of course. Like Kelly McGillis in "Top Gun", Leslie Easterbrook in "Police Academy" or Brigitte Nielsson in "Rocky IV".

The perfect woman had her own income, better if she owned her own company, stood up for herself, was bossy and made everybody do what she wanted, while having a family and being always seductive and in perfect shape.

The reality was, that men admired such strong women in movies but not as their real life-partner. Here the trouble began. In theory we were *told* to be strong girls, speak up and say what was on our minds. In reality that was *not OK*, especially for girls. At school we often had old teachers from the silent generation who had very traditional ideas about girls and boys and pupils in general. They were supposed to obey, otherwise they were in big trouble.

So we had a *theory*, taught by our parents, on TV in advertisement, but had no role models in real life.

On the other hand we have been frowned upon by the Silent Generation for being too unfeminine. *"You will never find a husband if you behave like a boy."* We had no clue what to do. Too many contrasting opinions.

In the end GenX women grew up to be strong and independent, some are divorced, almost all have a job or are looking one, even with children, mainly for financial reasons. We were told to not depend on *anyone* and that we *have* to do *everything:* job, kids, household and so on.

That's why most GenX women are juggling though their days, trying to manage it all. It's not OK anymore to be *only* a mom or *only* a housewife. We had to grow into some kind of superwoman without anybody showing us how to do that.

We were not supposed to be like our moms and neither like our grandmothers. We were supposed to be something new. That's why we tried to find some inspiration in the media, TV and magazines but the role models presented were not very helpful.

When we were teenagers in the 1990s and tried to find a female role model, we had to chose between television or magazines. All we had were airbrushed supermodels, just *looking* nice without having to say or *do* anything. The other models were the "anorexic-heroin-chic" with smokey eyes and sluggish posture, quite unrealistic to follow as well. What a great choice. We had no idea of how to behave as a girl or a boy and just went for it by trial and error. Today you can find millions of YouTube videos about dating, partnership and love life, every single problem is addressed and you can easily find answers to all your questions.

Even asking somebody on a date was an adventure. In a world without cell phones (they became popular only in the end of the 1990's) we had to look up the desired person on the actual *phone book*, finding their father's name and dial the number. If some other family member answered the phone, we had to tell them who we were and who we wanted to talk to. Quite embarrassing when it was their parents!

If the line was occupied or the person wasn't home, there was no way of telling him that you had called. If we wanted to talk to somebody or get noticed, we had to come up with an excuse or some idea to get the other person to like us in real life.

No Instagram stories or texts, no photo-shopped pictures or filters. Above all: no clue of how to present yourself to the opposite sex. Just trial and error, many embarrassing moments and lots of creative ideas.

Our grandparents had had a small booklet called "etiquette", a guideline of rules for manners.. They knew exactly what was adequate to say or to do. They knew how to talk and behave and had some cinematic role models to follow.

They knew how to say romantic phrases or be a gentleman or a lady. They could follow *schemes*, knew what to do and what the other person expected from them. It had all been written down.

The Baby Boomers disrupted this scheme with the idea of genders having equal rights and not to follow any of the old dating rules, so the idea of being a gentleman or a lady was widely frowned upon. But the Baby Boomers did know what rules there were to break in the the first place, they had *grown up* with them and had in mind what one was supposed to be doing and what not.

We were the first generation to grow up without *any* dating rules or better, very *contrary* rules, as a girl you were supposed to do all the things that boys did, but tragically that didn't work out either.

Our parents had decided to debate these topics as young adults, showing it was ok to stand up for ones rights and change the world.

But we were just *kids*.

We were fighting a gender war for *them*. Without having no clue what was happening. We have been instrumentalized. It was a big burden to be inbetween the two parts. The war was carried out on our backs.

Girls were told to be independent and boys were told... nothing! Some grew up in a divorced household with their single mom and without any male role model to learn from. Others in a world where both, the weak and the macho man were frowned upon. Contrasting advice also for the boys.

The role models in movies were Sylvester Stallone, Mr T. and Arnold Schwarzenegger, big strong guys on their own. No relationship advice at all. Not to much talking to anyone at all. So what was a young Gen X boy supposed to do? Trial and error, the feedback wasn't always as expected and it took some time to conquer somebody's heart.

Nowadays some Gen X couples still have trouble to understand each other. That's why there are so many books on the market today, giving relationship advice. Many are single or divorced and the old schemes of relationships simply don't apply anymore. Women know and show their man that they could go along perfectly without him, and men don't need women anymore to cook or do the household because they are perfectly capable of living on their own.

We don't *need* each other anymore, the old gender roles are outdated and we have to find a reason why we actually *want* to be with somebody. We all have to struggle much harder to make the basics work. In the 1950s and 1960s it was enough for the man to go to work and for the woman to take care of the household. With only one income a family could pay the bills and have a decent life.

Now all this is not enough anymore. We *all* need to have a job, and everybody has to take care of the household and children, have hobbies, a healthy body, a perfect wardrobe and a social life. Yes, of course a woman nowadays can have a job, but unlike her male counterpart she *also* has to take care of all the rest, or at least most of it anyway. I hardly know any couple where the housework is equally divided 50% 50%, even if both work the same hours. The woman almost always does much more.

So the equality that our mothers had in mind is still far from being reality. Theoretically equality was supposed to give the same worth and opportunities to both genders. One person at work and one at home. A woman was supposed to be able to work and her husband stay at home.

But that's not the case. If you want (or better have to be) a working woman, you will never ONLY have to work and come home to a clean home with a dinner waiting for you. You will always have to do both, unless you have a high payed job and can hire somebody for taking care of everything.

Also the male counterpart has changed. Rarely a family can afford a partner staying at home so they both have to work full-time jobs and both have to take care of the household *and* the kids. Some are single or divorced and have their job and the household.

The workload got more for both and in many cases couple have either no kids or in their late 30s or 40s because they don' t know where to leave the kids during work hours. Most cannot even allow to pay for a babysitter,even working both full time. That's why many have to rely on their parents to get along if they want to have a family. That's very depressing for both because they cannot even afford a family on their own even working twice as much.

Many Baby Boomers had children at a young age, the husband could provide for the family and even a divorced mother could get along with one income. Today man and women cannot provide for a family and take care of their young. It's frustrating.

On top of that the Baby Boomers still tell us, that we are losers because we are not even capable of having a family on our own, but still rely on *them. They* didn't have to rely on anybody, Daddy just worked very hard and they made *sacrifices* and *that's* why they could live on their own.

The generations today cannot even *live* without their help. *"See, I always told you that you couldn't get your life together, you're worth nothing without me. When I was your age, I could do it all, but younger generations are no good at doing anything."*

OK Boomer (cit), this is not because we don't *want* to, it's because with all your political choices we are covered in *your* debts. We cannot have one parent stay at home or pay a nanny because we have to pay off the debts *you* left us. How? In taxes. We are also paying for *your* retirement. Oh yes, because you have worked for 40 years so you *deserve* it. You know what *we* will receive after 40 years of work? Another 15-20 years of work and then *nothing*. Because we don't *deserve* it? No, because you've used up all the money there was. But you already know that, the Millennials tell you all the time.

Back to gender roles:

Nowadays you can observe many Gen X-couples, in real life and movies (especially comedies) where the woman is very confident and strong and the man doesn't really know what to do. And all movie long he tries to do new, funny and unpredictable things to make her happy and accept him.

If you remember the sitcoms "How I met your Mother" or "The Big Bang Theory" you see the difference between the genders: All girls are confident and know what they want, but the men don't know where to start. Baby Boomer men just suggest to be a macho but GenXers know exactly that that won't work with GenX girls. They try to be kind, understanding, unpredictable, funny and some of the tricks they learned from their grandfather or uncle.

The definition of male and female in the GenX world is so confusing that it really is not easy to make a relationship work.

In the old, traditional system, roles were strict and defined. Surely not right, but easy to follow. We instead had to find new ways to communicate and make our partner and ourselves happy. We know that the antique role definition doesn't work in modern society and the divorce rates of Baby Boomers proved this theory to be right.

So we keep on trying to do our best in life by trial and error. Some GenX men and -women in the end just don't care anymore.

They stay single because they don't want all the hustle of building a relationship and a family because they have been hurt or just find it all to confusing. Why should I try to do all that and then maybe she/he will walk away on me again?

That's not worth it.

The previous generations built their self-esteem on their house, family and children.

GenXers can be perfectly happy without that.

We don't need to prove anything to anybody.

18 JUST GO AHEAD AND DO IT

We GenXers grew up self sufficient and independent. We don't lose ourselves in endless monologues. We are the are the *Doers*. We just *do* things, without bragging about it, complaining or in many cases even taking credit for it.

The job needs to be done, and we go for it. GenXers are result-orientated. We don't believe in hierarchy. We don't want anybody to tell *us*, neither tell anybody *else* what to do. We grew up without adults being around all the time to entertain us, guide us through step by step or do things for us. We tried. We invented things, failed, tried again and again.

51% of all start-ups are founded by GenXers Many have innovative ideas, plenty have started their own business, most are independent workers. If you give a GenXer a task, just walk away and when you come back he/she'll be done with it. We like to be left alone for thinking and trying, we are used to get along on our own.

That's why be don't believe in hierarchy. Everybody on his own, no boss and no followers. That's baby Boomers' stuff. But strangely Millennials *like* hierarchy, they want to climb the ladder, be more important and count more than others. That's why companies have come up with fancy names, like "Manager of economics" for a cashier or "Head responsible of recycling" for the employee who changes the waste bins. They crave for attention, they want to feel important. For us it's crazy, but if that makes you feel a better person, go ahead. We can call you whatever you want but that doesn't change who you are or what you do.

If you have a GenXer boss he/she most probably will explain you what he wants and leave. He guesses that also you can figure it out by yourself. That's where many Millennials find themselves in trouble, they need the feedback all the time. Want to know if they are doing right, they want to be guided. We GenXers don't understand that part and for many of us it's strange at work to have to give feedback all the time to younger co-workers. We just take the task and DO it, we don't need anyone's opinion or approval. If we mess up, we stand up for it. The sports brand Nike™ in 1988 came up with the best slogan ever: "just do it" .

That's perfect for us. No fuzzing around, no excuses, no endless discussions. We don't even get what feedback is good for. I can understand ranking and customer ratings, but feedback? We grew up in a world where there was no such thing: We grew up *watching* television, a one way communication.

No interaction. No "comment section" on YouTube where you can let the author know that you liked or hated his channel. No "Yahoo answers" and no "Google search". There was no interaction at all.. Nobody would explain anything. We were merely spectators behind a thick glass wall, we couldn't interact at all, ask questions or go back and watch it again. Once had passed, it was gone forever. No YouTube videos to stop and watch again, no pause on Netflix. So we had to be alert and pay attention and if we hadn't understood something we had to be lucky to have friends or siblings around (who would mostly make something up because they hadn't understood anything either.)

And if we disagreed with anything, well that was *our* problem. No customer satisfaction inquiry, no smileys to rate the service. If we were unhappy with something we could tell our friends, but that was all. Surely, we could try to send a handwritten letter to the film company to state our disapproval but hardly anybody would read it and for sure you would never get a response.

Unlike the Baby Boomers or the Millennials who constantly feel the urge to share their opinion about everyone and everything ceaselessly, GenXers mostly don't. We don't see the point.

Only if it's something of utmost importance. Then we try to stick to the facts and don't make it very long. That, on the other hand, scares the other generations.

They are used to *us* being *silent*, but when we *do* speak up it can be very painful and direct. They talk all the time and give their opinion about any topic, but the minute *we* say something, they get very upset and defensive.

We study our conversational partner, we listen and we think. We might let it go. But if they really say something off, we might state our opinion, very direct and true. We can be painfully honest and destructive. So if you can't handle the truth you better not ask a GenXer for his/her opinion.

We are often accused of being cynical. I find that amusing. Of course we are. We are pragmatic, realistic and unlike the later Generations, we have witnessed so many ideas rise and fall that we've become very skeptical towards miracles. We were born into the mess of an after party and we knew that we would have been the ones, to clean it all up. We have been disillusioned over and over again. So we deeply distrust society. We have been given shitty jobs, other generations take credit for our inventions and we are even called "Boomers" by some Millennials or Zoomers because they don't even know who we are.

We've been screwed over so many times and the world calls us slackers. We are so tired of the self-centered generations that we are stuck in between and that know it all better. Yes we are deeply cynical and that's a good thing. It's our way to survive. There was not much optimism around when we grew up. We are realists and you have to admit that our deep distrust of everything turned out to be 100% correct.

We have learned to think outside the box when we were kids. So we've tried lots of new ideas and we pretty much know what works and what doesn't. If you have a new project we'll analyze it and then approve or disapprove. GenXers hardly get all excited for a new idea, they mostly stay cool and think it through.

But then they commit, work on it and just go ahead and DO it, without having to make millions of meetings or early conclusions. Only time will proof if an idea is worthy.

19. FASHION

As young teens in the 1980s and 1990s we grew up with the feeling of not being good enough because on television everybody was so perfect and we weren't like that in real life.

We were bombarded by professional pictures taken by super photographers of supermodels in the perfect lighting, makeup and location. The pictures had also been *airbrushed* before send to print. The only role models in beauty we had were impossible to achieve.

'Supermodels' were very popular in the 1990s: Naomi Campbell 1970, Cindy Crawford 1966, Claudia Schiffer 1970, Linda Evangelista 1965, Heidi Klum 1973 and so on.

Today we can watch tutorials on YouTube on "how to dress for your body type" and "apply make up even on hooded eyes". That's such a help! Of course people use Instagram filters and heavy make up, but at least there's an idea of what people look like in real life.

In the beginning of make-up-tutorials the gurus are without any makeup and you're like "wow, *that's* what I look like, too without make-up"!

Today everybody can post pictures of *themselves* on social media. There are reality shows and live chats, even the models themselves talking about their beauty regime, diet, workout or make up. During Lock-down we could see celebrities in their sweat-pants at home, without their make-up artist and the perfect lighting. We can see real people in real life, not only airbrushed models on TV or magazines. In the 1990s that's all we had.

Fast fashion didn't exist yet and clothes were not very even flattering but still expensive. No Jeggins or nice basics at cheap fashion stores. If we wanted to dress decently we had to spend lots of money and the result wasn't even that great. Women wore mainly unisex clothes: smaller men's jeans which were really stiff and were not cut for girls, like LEVIS 501. Loose T-shirts, basically small men's cuts, and also combat boots like Dr.Martens which have had a great comeback last year.

Mainly square, boxy clothes and open flannel shirts over a white T-shirt. Hiding any curve. That was very far from what we saw in the sitcoms on TV, but we had no idea on how to achieve perfect waves, glamorous make-up or how to dress a pear shaped body.

We simply tried on all kind of clothes and played with make-up, if we wanted professional help, again, we had to take an expensive course on "which colors matched our skin tone", how to "assemble an outfit" or all the small make-up tricks and tips that are so easily available on YouTube today.

Here again, our perseverance and patience were fundamental, we had to try lots and lots of combinations of clothes. We've spend hours in front of the mirror to try hairstyles that never worked or recreate looks we had seen on MTV. But in the end we just assumed that we were all ugly, fat, not tanned enough, with terrible skin and hair, because in real life nobody looked as great as the celebrities. There were no pictures of celebs without make-up. They were always perfect. The 1980s had been the era of athletic people, like Arnold Schwarzenegger and films about sports like "Rocky", "Karate Kid", "Teen Wolf", "Flashdance" and even "Police Academy" were en vogue.

Then the 1990s promoted very skinny and anorexic boys and girls (trainspotting like) and the new tendency towards "heroin chic" was born. Models on advertisements looked like broken dolls, very dark with smeared make up. Some famous female band's lead singers, like "Skin" - the lead singer of "Skunk Anansie" (1967) and also "Sinead O'Connor"(1966) had both shaved heads.

Even "Dolores O'Riordan" (1971) - lead singer of "The Cranberries" didn't have a long, wavy, seductive mane, but a very short pixie cut.

Femininity was not defined by being pretty and sweet anymore, but by being skinny, angry and kind of self-destructive. Clothes were boxy and stiff, girls were mostly dressed in androgynous outfits and far from being elegant or sexy. Girls were supposed to be strong and powerful, not elegant and ladylike.

Every country had its own style and on holidays we could tell right away what country people came from, based on their outfits and the brands they used. "Birkenstock" shoes were worn only by Germans, Italy had "Kappa" and "Fila"- Jumpsuits and only British girls would wear combat boots in combination with dresses. Today with globalization, social media and fast fashion, we can see the same outfits, hairstyles and make-up in all countries. They all look like the pictures on Instagram or Pinterest.

When I look back at pictures from the 1990s I can state very confidently that nowadays we dress and look much better. Had I only had the clothes and possibilities back then! We had no idea how to dress, wear make-up or do our hair. We tried to copy celebrities or people we knew but never understood why somethings looked great on them and terrible on us.

Now with "color analysis" and "body-types" things make finally sense. Some outfits couldn't look good on us, because they would not fit our skin-tone or body type. Also decent clothes were difficult to find. If we wanted a piece of clothing in a plain, basic color without all the crazy prints, we had to turn to the expensive brands. Cheap stuff was full of prints and patterns.

I am so glad that finally today we can get decent basics at a reasonable price, that has taken forever! I am not saying that fast fashion is a good thing, but it must be possible for every budget to get the basics for a decent capsule wardrobe. In the 1990s that was almost impossible.

Lately I have seen some of the 1990s style coming back: flannel shirts, Dr.Martens and boxier clothing. But the material is so much nicer to the touch and figure flattering that they look better today! LOL.

Well, every decade has its fashion, I guess we will laugh about 2020 outfits in 2050 as well. Or the same fashion might just have a great comeback, as it always does.

20. PARENTING

Women of the Greatest and the Silent generation had no choice but stay at home with their children, once married. Divorce or abortion was never an option, at least not legally of course.

Baby Boomers instead grew up in a changing society. Women were asked to join the work force due to economic growth and they started to claim their share. Now women's rights were discussed openly, so divorce and abortion became important topics. The Baby Boomers were part of a new generation that still had their children at a young age but besides that, wanted more. Parent self-realization was the key.

Before the industrialization people had to work in the fields or at other very physically demanding jobs and there was no such thing as 'spare-time' for the poor and middle classes.

In the 1970s and 1980s 'hobbies' suddenly became popular among working classes. Everybody was supposed to join also social activities, besides their jobs and family. Entertainment, 'Do it yourself' and many new hobbies were invented. Hobbies that involved spending *money*. The production of goods and services had to rise. So new desires were created: a special attire and gear for the latest sport, professional brushes for painting, films and cameras for photography etc. People in the 1980s were obsessed with their hobbies.

So here we were, the first GenXers, children of young 20 year-old that wanted to do anything with their lives but just being a parent.

Children were often perceived as a disturbing factor and if somebody came to babysit, our parents told *us children* to behave. *'Don't create any trouble to the nice person who is so kind to watch you'.*

Today's babysitters have a 'babysitter diploma' and parents are worried that the babysitter might not be the perfect choice for the *kids*. The other way around.

From the mid 1980s to the late 1990s the *Millennials* were born. They were either children of the first GenXers or children of elder Baby Boomers that for some reason had their babies later in their lives. Something interesting happened.

Millennials were raised completely differently. They were either elder Baby Boomers' long desired children or the first of GenXers that wanted to give their offspring more attention than they had received growing up.

Suddenly parents were highly *interested* in their kids, praising them all the time. I remember my Gen X friend who had her children in her 20s in the early 1990s. She had a list of "100 ways to praise your child" on her fridge: "Well done! good job! Excellent!" So instead of being a disturbing factor in somebody's life now children became the *center* of all the attention. They were pampered and supported continuously and praised for very little effort.

Another very important thing changed here as well: parents became the main source of *entertainment.* When we GenXers were kids, we were send out to play alone or watched TV by ourselves. When we got bored we had to find something to do on our own. We know *real* boredom. I mean *real boredom.* Nothing interesting to do at *all.* But that made us creative.

Millennials instead grew up with round-the-clock entertainment and attention. If today other generations blame them for being egocentric and putting themselves always first, well, that's what they grew up with. Today they are in their late 20s to mid 30s and you can notice the difference by *how* they use social media. They grew up with parents entertaining them constantly, asking for their opinion, praising them and letting them know that they were important and desired perpetually.

Today we see Millennials all over the socials, posting *selfies* and filming their *own faces* in boomerang (ain't I pretty?) Many are desperately counting "likes" (which translate into praises) to feed their ego.

Most grew up with ceaselessly attention and as soon as it fades away, they become very insecure and question everything. As if they were asking *"Does nobody like me anymore? Give me your attention!"* Many Millennials need constant recognition, also in their jobs. I know many that want to be walked through every little step and need constant positive feedback to know that they are doing OK. Very different from what we grew up with.. I don't blame them, I am not blaming anybody.

I just want to find out *why* some behavior patterns repeat throughout the generations, to help us understand each other. It's not their fault. But excuse us GenXers if we roll our eyes if you want our eternal attention. Just find yourself something to do and leave us alone. LOL.

I noticed that many Millennials felt destroyed when they turned 30. And I know that it was a big thing when the first Baby Boomers turned 50. It was in the newspapers, on TV, big discussion everywhere. But we GenXers? Nothing. We don't care either. We just carry on with our lives and our hobbies as if nothing had happened Have you seen Jennifer Lopez performing at the super ball? She turned 50 last year! But she just keeps on doing what she loves. And she looks amazing.

Just like JLO herself, many GenXers had their children later in their lives, the largest group of children of almost exclusively GenXers is Gen Z. Born between the late 90s and 2015. Gen Z was raised more independent, with very clear ideas in their minds and a quite realistic view of the world. Some call them the "old young people" for they seem to be quite calm and down-toned in their way of dressing and opinion. Most grew up watching their parents struggle with the real life's problems, recall the global economic crisis after 2008. They know today's life's problems but also look for new solutions.

There's a theory that "noisy" generations alternate with "silent" ones. That's why the Baby Boomers have a lot in common with the Millennials. That's the reason they fight all the time. Their behavior is quite similar, even if they grew up in a different period of time. They are both demanding, self centered and take everything personally. Both always have to win the argument.

On the other hand they are the GenXers and Gen Z, more quiet and less "aggressive" in their overall behavior. They don't want to change *people* but the *world*. The Swedish activist Greta Thunberg for example doesn't attack people personally, but accuses their behavior as a group.

The chief engineer and CEO of Tesla Elon Musk (1971) tries to save the planet - or at least mankind - by colonizing mars, with his creative work. He doesn't attack people all day long but uses his energy to find solutions.

Both generations, Gen X and Gen Z adapted two different survival strategies:

Gen X became independent, interacting in small groups or on their own and perceive themselves as individuals. Many don't want to belong to a a group to or don't care.

Gen Z on the other hand, acts as a *collective*, they understand that they are connected, probably due to the internet and socials, and move as a crowd.

I wonder what Generation Alpha (born after 2015) will be like. If the pattern repeats they will grow into another "loud" generation.
Let's see what happens.

Only time can tell.

21. POSSESSION

Most members of the silent generation have experienced poverty when they were young. They grew up during the great depression 1929-1939 and WWII 1939-1945 when people used to live on very little with many children and hardly any possessions.

Things were often handcrafted by people, not machines, clothing by tailors, furniture was built to last and family possessions were passed down through generations. If something broke you've got it fixed, people wore darned socks and clothing, furniture was repaired and craftsmanship highly valued.

But then something shifted: with the early 1950s and 1960s capitalism had its boom in the western countries and consumerism was promoted. New advertising campaigns were invented to make people consume more, necessities were *created* and *emotions* sold to the costumer.

You didn't buy something because you really *needed* it but because you *wanted* it. And if you didn't have the money you could get credit and buy the item with small monthly payments. Debt was created for the small people, even the average person could buy anything right away. No need to save money first. Deferred gratification was converted into *instant* gratification. Baby Boomers were the first children to grow up with the concept of *'get it now - pay later!'*

People from the Silent Generation were still used to keep, store and repair their possession. But now they had the possibility to *also* buy all the new products. Most of them were very concerned of not spending too much and always keeping something 'just in case'. We all know some elder peoples' homes with old candies and ancient, even cracked or broken items, but they never throw *anything* away, because you 'never know'.

The have lived poverty and know that in hard times of rationalization you have to rely on things that you have accumulated during the years in your own home. We have experienced a fraction of that reality during Covid 19 lock down when toilet paper wasn't available anymore in supermarkets.

The Baby Boomers instead were children and teens in the 1950s and 1960s. They knew all the *stories* about poverty and they had *been taught* not to throw away anything. Meanwhile they grew up in an advertised world. They love to buy *and* accumulate things. In the 1980s and 1990s products became cheaper with mass production.

Most of our toys and clothes had already been produced in Asia but by an expensive western brand, so automatically considered to be of 'high quality'.

Today media talk about 'made in china' as if it was synonymous of 'low quality' just because the prices went down. Until western companies made all the profit they were considered 'quality items' and now 'cheap'. Interesting indeed.

Baby Boomers were the first (and only) to live consumerism to the fullest. They could also afford to do so economically. When a Silent Generation-er wants to show you his love he will give you *food*. When a Baby Boomer wants to show you their affection, it's through *items*. The more you have the better.

We as kids grew up with a lot of stuff, lots of things and cluttered homes. The advertisement always told us that we would be happier buying new stuff and own things, but we already knew that this couldn't be true.

We were standing in the land of abundance, staring into the abyss.

That's why GenXers show their affection through *time*. We do something for you. We make you a playlist. We spend time with you or create something for you. Anybody smiling? So you know what I'm talking about :)

Many GenXers still hold on to their possessions, because our grandparents have cemented this concept in our brains and that's very hard to overcome.

But some, especially the later GenXers, Xennilas and Millennials follow the new discovered trend of *minimalism*. There's nothing new to the idea of minimalism, but in the past decades with heavy consumerism we have accumulated way to much clutter and stuff that just fills our homes and makes us feel overwhelmed and guilty. They want to free ourselves from all the possessions that don't really make us happy and keep only what we actually use.

There are many books and blogs by famous Xennials and Millennials like "the life-changing magic of tidying up" by Marie Kondo (1984) or "Minimalism - live a meaningful life" by "the minimalists" Ryan Nicodemus (1981) and Joshua Fields Millburn (1981). They explain how *not* buying any unnecessary items and keep it simple is the key to happiness and joy.

Many Millennials also adopted the idea of " YOLO" - "you only live once". Instead of accumulating possession many prefer adventure and exiting trips around the world. There are also two important factors making that choice easier, one is that with today's low cost flights it is easier to see new places and the second is that there is less *necessity* to keep everything, because with fast fashion and cheap items available you can replace things very quick and easily.

Where previously we had to scan many shops and wait for the right product, now you can just order online with a click, everything is always available and there are no hard times because supply hardly ever finishes.

Except for toilet paper during Covid 19. LOL. That was the fist time for many to realize that there *is* actually a supply chain and it *can* also be interrupted. Lock-down made us reflect and reconsider possession and necessary versus superfluous items in our homes.

Minimalism is also a way to address the economic crisis, we have to think more of where our money goes because it is easy to accumulate debt.

Even though items like clothing have become cheaper, life in general has become more expensive.

GenXers are somewhere in between, many love the idea of less cluttered homes but be still hold onto things. We become attached to our car, computer or stereo.

We don't necessarily try to fix things, but many of us when they buy a new item don't let go of the old. Many have adopted the minimalist idea but we still have a hard time letting things go. It was repeated so many times by the elder generations to keep things 'just in case' that we have to overcome those voices in our heads. It doesn't come natural to us, we actually have to work through it.

Even if today we can get all the music online, I bet most GenXers still have their CD collection somewhere. Got you! It's not only about the music, it's the cover, the moment we bought that CD in a store and the first time we listened to it. Some GenXers consider themselves fiscally conservative but socially liberal.

Most Gen Z instead grew up with 'sharing'. They enjoy movies and music online, car sharing and other services but without 'owning' the item. They don't need to buy the CD, DVD or electric scooter, they just pay for *using* it. That's a completely new approach to possession. They don't pay for the physical *item* but just the *access for a limited amount of time.*

This reminds me of "Imagine" by John Lennon (1971):

"Imagine no possessions, I wonder if you can, no need for greed or hunger, a brotherhood of man, imagine all the people, sharing all the world".

His prediction might become reality with new technologies. We already share information, knowledge and services online. Now also material things like cars, scooters, and other items.

Less need to spend time, money and worries on our possessions.

More time and money to enjoy life.

22. ENVIRONMENT

Just close your eyes for a minute and think about the 1970s and 1980s and the environment. Not such a healthy picture. Cars still used lead based gasoline until 1996, households loved to buy plastic disposable plates and cutlery. Companies added as much chemicals to food and clothes as they wanted (hardly any regulations there) and schools were built with asbestos to prevent fire.

The idea of "saving the planet" was mainly laughed at as 'annoying tree hugger stuff' and 'foolish hippy ideas'. Fossil energy was still the main source of energy and many children suffered from chronic coughs due to the emissions of coal-based power plants.

The industrialized nations tried to come up with a better alternative and that was thought to be *nuclear energy*. From 1954 on they started building nuclear power plants across the USSR, US, Europe and many other industrialized countries.

'Pro nuclear' ads were everywhere for the new, fantastic and clean power and it was thought to be perfect and save. We had yellow stickers with a winking smiling sun claiming *'nuclear power - of course'*. As kids we hoped that maybe our future could be better with clean energy to fuel cars. Without petrol and no more cancer due to fossil combustion.

But then, on April 26th 1986 the Chernobyl nuclear power plant close to the city of Pripyat (in today's Ukraine) in what at the time was the Soviet Union, had caused one of the worst nuclear environmental disasters in the world.

Several explosions blew off the reactor's lid and released large amounts of radioactive material into the atmosphere. A radioactive cloud passed over Belarus, Russia, Ukraine and Europe. Millions of acres of forest and farmland were contaminated, livestock born deformed and radiation induced cancers deaths were expected in the long term.

We were still kids, but we knew that we had to live with the consequences of that disaster for all our lives. Once again we were blown away by the world of the grown ups. It seemed that they were playing with our planet and our future and with dangerous toys they had no idea about what they were capable of. For some month in Europe we were not allowed to play outside or touch the sand, eat fruits, vegetables or mushrooms that year.

We were terrified, because radioactivity cannot be seen, heard or smelled. It was just there in the air like a strange virus ready to kill us all.

In the years to come there were always some kids from the Ukraine who came to Western Europe on "detox holidays" for some weeks. They were just small kids like us and the grown ups said that every *week* spent with us (away from radioactivity) would add a *year* to their life expectancy. War was over but also our parent's generation did their part to put our lives in danger. The Cold War was at its peak but we didn't care where the threat came from, the radioactivity was going to be there forever and maybe it was time to think as a *planet* and not as individual nations. Radioactive clouds don't respect boarders.

Only three years later, in March of 1989 another environmental disaster struck the planet. One of the worst human caused environmental disasters in recent history. I remember vividly the videos of birds and fish covered in the black oil by "Exxon Valdez". This huge oil tanker had struck the Prince William Sound Bligh reef in Alaska and leaked 10,8 million US Gallons of crude oil into the ocean. Everything was covered in a thick layer of oil, dead bodies of fish and birds floated on the surface and the view was horrifying.

We just couldn't believe that this was caused by humans. In the news they talked about this for weeks. The greed for money of the companies and the non existing safety rules made one disaster happen after another. We couldn't believe it, again our planet had been struck by one of the dangerous toys of the grown ups.

If now every three years a disaster like this would hit the planet, then *nature* for us and the generations to come would simply not be existing in the future. Neither to live from nor to exploit as our parents' generation was doing. Why were they doing this? For money. Money that was not invested in the *future* but for personal desire.

Debt was rising and rising and even nuclear power plants or oil tankers that polluted the oceans wouldn't stop that trend. Only some private companies had gained big profits whereas the health of the planet and the people was completely set aside. Nobody seemed to care for the future, the health of the planet or us children. It never crossed their minds that they were destroying also *our* future, *our* health and *our* planet. They had inherited the earth from their parents so now they were convinced to be entitled to do with it whatever they wanted.

It was the late 1980s, when many GenXers were still teens, when we collectively decided that we were *not* going be like our parent's generation. We didn't want to be as greedy and careless as them. Even though in some European countries recycling and reusing of garbage started in the late 1980s, most adults didn't care.

Now in the last 30 years finally progress has been made and people started caring more and more about the environment. It has taken a lot of protests, awareness campaigns and work to get to this point. We've started as kids to use less energy and wanted a cleaner future, some of us work in the renewable energy resources but the big power companies are still using coal and nuclear power to produce energy.

Baby Boomers had decided in the 1980s that they would not use coal-based power plants anymore in 2040 in some countries. Isn't that interesting. They didn't quit *earlier,* that would have meant lot less money for their pockets.

2040 was 60 years from the 80s. 2040 meant that they would all be in their 80s and 90s. Until that day they wanted to make *profit* regardless of the cancers that causes and environmental problems. Exploit the planet until the end. *Their* end. Who cares what happens after they are gone?

Most GenXers, Millennials and Gen Z as consumers pay lots of attention to the label, we want to choose the better option, we know that we, as consumers, can change something. Finally today there are more bio products, healthy options and informative choices. It is compulsory to print all the ingredients, nutrition value and country of origin.

But it is not enough. Airplanes still work as they did in the 60s, cars have changed only in terms of safety but little in terms of consuming. Still in 2020 we are using petrol to drive our cars, like in the 1950s. They eliminated only lead from gas in 1996, but the rest stayed the same. Cars pretty much consume the same amount of gas as they did 30 years ago.

There have always been many prototypes of electric cars, the first one was invented in 1890. Isn't that amazing? Electric cars had been invented 100 earlier, yet the marked only produced cars that ran on gas. Only now, in 2020 there are the first hybrid cars on the marked for the masses. Where have they been all these years? Why didn't the market let us choose what we wanted to drive or offer new alternatives of transportation?

Still today we have the same problems as in the 1970s and 1980s, smog and pollution. We are more people on the planet, consuming always more resources. Finally some GenXers have come up with new business ideas, car-sharing by app and low carbon footprint production.

Leonardo DiCaprio (1974), for example, has launched a Foundation in 1998 at the age of 24 "dedicated to the protection and well being of all earth's inhabitants". He also co-invested, together with Biz Stone and Evan Williams (remember the founders of Twitter?) and other celebrities in the creation of "beyond meat", a vegan alternative to meat, reducing 87% of the carbon footprint.

Also many Millennials and Gen Z promote this way of reducing waste and sharing things. Physical items have been replaced by online services that provide music, series and movies for free or a flat rate. They will be always less stuff to clutter our homes, less things, paperwork, books and documents. Most are online, available through cloud or accessible through the app on our phones. Much less stuff to physically own, collect, clean and take care of. Nature will profit from this too, because there will be less production of items that eventually, one day, inevitably will end up in some landfill.

Slowly we are trying to make our way to a healthier environment. I am glad that Greta Thunberg brought up the topic and finally at least people are listening to her. Many others tried the same but it never worked.

Leonardo DiCaprio was already a superstar in 2007 when he published the documentary "the 11th hour" about the imminent environmental problems. But sadly, despite the fact that he was famous, very few people ever watched that movie.

Without smart phones or social media it was much harder to reach people. I remember protesting against a big trash incinerator close to my city with self made cardboard signs, but there was nobody to take pictures. No newspaper wrote about it and no TV station would have ever talked about it. We tried to do our best, recycle garbage, use environmental friendly products and consume less water and energy. But we didn't have the means to spread our message as today.

Most CEOs and presidents of corporations were still Baby Boomers and the only thing that we could control was our *consumer* behavior. But there were hardly any "better" options to chose from. It was very hard to get information about where products came from, how they were made and if there was any animal testing involved.

Today thanks to Google, Wikipedia and YouTube anybody can go viral and spread their message easily. We can research any product and chose from a wide range of vegan, cruelty free and recyclable options. Thanks to our decisions the market now offers products for everyone and there are compulsory labels on packages.

GenXers actually *have* changed the world. Not using guns or violence, burning cars or houses. We did it without using violence or hate. By inventing means to spread our message and making choices as consumers. Inventing eco-friendly products.

So don't tell us we didn't do anything because that's simply not true. Our revolution is like us, patient and humble: step by step we created a new market, we forced the industries to provide "green" choices and invented lots of new products and services that makes life so much easier for everyone.

We were patient, persistent and creative. The world is surely not a perfect place but if many things have become so much easier in the past 20 years that's also thanks to us. But you will never know it was Generation X, we don't brag about our achievements, remember?

23. NUCLEAR PARANOIA

In the 1970s and 1980s the political map was still shifting. The war in Vietnam had just ended in 1975 and the Cold War was at its peak with the Western world against the Eastern block. The northern world was split into 2 parts: USA against the USSR, divided by the famous "Iron Curtain".

New weapons were tested, nuclear missiles were placed everywhere and we had learned about the "overkill" in school. The nations could practically kill everybody on the whole planet with all the weapons that they had put up against each another not only *once* but *several* times. Thanks to film producers we had vivid images, as in Terminator 1984 and many other movies that gave us nightmares with the computer animated outcome of a nuclear overkill.

We were living with the knowledge that *war* was a terrible thing, never to happen again, but also that there would be no WW3 because the whole planet would just be blown up by nuclear bombs. The fear that one day somebody could launch the first bomb by mistake and they would all follow each other, wiping out every life form on earth, was omnipresent. There is a famous song by German pop star Nena called "99 Luftballons" ("99 red balloons" that ranked number 1 in the US charts, Europe and Japan in 1983) which describes this exact scenario:

"99 red balloons flying peacefully over the horizon, but military thinks it's an attack from out of space and sends fighter jets to take them down. The enemy mistakes this for declaration to war. The war goes on for 99 years and in the end nothing is left but one red balloon floating silently over the ashes of the world."

We all feared that this could happen, anything trivial could trigger a nuclear war and we would all die. Europe was divided in two parts, the western world under NATO and the eastern as the Soviet Union. GenXers growing up in the eastern part of the world were also called "The last soviet children" who grew up behind the Iron Curtain.

Right in the heart of the conflict the country of Germany, divided in 4 parts: the Allies (USA, UK and France) in the West and the Soviets in the eastern fraction. There was not only a wall but a whole "death zone" dividing the ex capital city of Berlin. We knew that the war wasn't actually *over*, that's why it was called "the Cold War". It was merely a *ceasefire*, but a peace contract had never been signed.

I grew up in a small town in Western Germany, a couple hundred yards from the Dutch border and we lived close to a NATO and a RAF (British Royal Air Force) airbase.

Our part of the country was in the British Sector. We were used to see jet fighters over our heads everyday, making exercises and breaking the sound barrier now and then with a great "booooooooooooooooooooooooommmmmmmmmm"!

They flew very low due to the flat landscape and we could recognize the planes by their sound without even looking up to the sky.

NATO planes flew usually higher and had a big radar on top to scan the landscape. The famous 'mushroom'. Everybody was so familiar to the jets speeding by at an extra low altitude, that the pilots joked *"if the cows don't turn tilt their heads, you are in flying in the right region"*.

Having a British air base nearby made us also live first hand the sad problems of the Northern Ireland conflict between the UK and Northern Ireland 1968 until 1998. Most British Soldiers and their families lived on base but others preferred living among civilians. Sadly there had often been reported victims of "IRA" - Provisional Irish Republican Army- attacks. Many times we passed by a house or a car that had blown up the night before, on our way to school.

On May 27 1990 in the nearby city of Roermond in the Netherlands, two Australian tourists, Nick Spanos and Stephen Melrose were traveling with in a British-registered car with their wife and girlfriend. Leaving the Italian Restaurant they had dined at, three gunmen sped up in their car and attacked with automatic weapons. The Australian Tourists had been shot dead by the IRA because they had been mistaken for British soldiers off duty. It was very sad and horrifying. For many month in the central market square of Roermond we saw flowers and candles to remember the victims.

We grew up fearing that the war could come back alive at any time and we were paralyzed by the idea. The Eastern part of Europe was under control of The Soviet Union. Most people were not allowed to leave their countries and were living under a strict communistic regime. On the other side, in the West, capitalism and consumerism was promoted.

The northern world was divided in two, not only politically but also ideologically, two opposite life styles and regimes. There was an endless battle to proof that each system was better that the other by launching rockets and shuttles into space and trying to win the race by advancing in technology.

On January 28th of 1986 the whole western world was ready to watch the launch of NASA's *Challenger*, into space. A space shuttle that was supposed to launch for the 10th time, but this time, onboard, besides the NASA crew carried also a a teacher: *Christa McAuliffe*.

She was supposed to give lessons from space. We were fascinated by the idea and thought that technology had made a giant leap. We were dreaming of traveling into space and floating around the earth. Sure that once we would have been adults, technology would have had developed so far that we could travel in space on holidays and have flying cars.

It took some days, the mission was delayed several times, but in the end finally here we were, witnessing the future. Our parents had seen the first man on the moon on TV and we were about to follow the first civilian in space. We felt so excited and thrilled by the idea to finally witness something cool, too.

The Shuttle took off at 11.39 EST so in western Europe it was quite late. But for this special occasion it was OK to stay up and watch the first teacher fly into space.

The adults were having a small party and we as kids were allowed to watch the take off in our pajamas before going to bed. We were all watching the launch in television, taking off beautifully. We were amazed by its power and felt the moment to be so special. We were witnessing the future of mankind. A teacher was flying into space and we were watching her live on TV.

But after only 73 seconds from take off, the space shuttle suddenly caught fire and finished in a big explosion right in front of our eyes. Shattered, we observed all the pieces and debris falling out of the sky into the Atlantic Ocean.

We were shocked. I'm sure that most of GenXers remember that day, we were mostly kids in school and just witnessed a teacher die in front of our eyes. Maybe technology wasn't so advanced as they had made us believe. Maybe the race for being the first in everything between the East and the West had reached its peak and the technicians were forced to do everything faster than would have been save. We didn't know.

But we have lost a little bit of faith in technology that day. In the mid 1980s the myth of he US against the Soviet Union was in many movies, even those that had nothing to do with a political plot, for example Rocky IV where the heavyweight champion of the US, Rocky Balboa, fights against his enemy Ivan Drago, the champion of the East.

Many spy- and action movies were based on the US against the USSR and even in many songs we were reminded of the East against the West. Like "Heroes" (by David Bowie in 1977), "Russians" (by Sting in 1985), "Leningrad" (by Billy Joel in 1989), and "Nikita" (by Elton

John in 1985), just to name a few. In those years, all over the world many different countries fought for their independence and separated mainly from western Europe (the UK, France; Portugal etc): Angola, 1975, Antigua and Bermuda 1981, Bahamas 1973, Bangladesh, 1971, Brunei 1984, Bulgaria 1978, Belize 1981 Cape Verde 1975, Comoros 1975, Dominica 1978 and so on. The political map in the South of the planet was changing while remaining quite static in the Northern half. The Cold War had grown very *cold* with fixed, sharply controlled borders and the political parts were set.

Then on October, 9th 1989 the Berlin Wall began to crumble and on October 3rd 1990 Germany was reunited. The Soviet Union was dissolved one year later in December of 1991. Some countries gained back their original borders, many had to fight for their independence. Also in Ex Yugoslavia a terrible civil war started from 1991 until 2001 with several countries fighting to get back their old independence and borders.

We observed a world changing from being "static"with fixed, severely controlled borders in the Cold War into a new world, with new countries, borders and laws. Old ideological thinking was replaced by economic preferences.

Growing up in the 1990s we saw a lot of changes also in society. First some countries were enemies, than friends, countries united and they divided back into smaller countries, nations and flags added to the map.

In my parent's house we used to have (and they still have) a huge political map with all the flags of the world in on the lower section. Almost every year it was outdated because new countries were established and others gained back their independence. It was constantly changing, the world that we had grown up in, did no longer exist. Countries went from communism to capitalism and old enemies became friends. In other countries families fought each other in a civil war. Anything could happen every day. The Olympic games had 1617 athletes from 149 countries in 1988 but only 4 years later in 1992 witnessed a boom of 9094 athletes from 172 countries. It was unbelievable.

For the German reunification in 1990, the rock band "Scorpions" released a song called "Wind of Change". Translating into music the change that was gusting through Europe:

"did you ever think that we could be so close like brothers"

"distant memories are buried in the past forever"

"the future's in the air I can feel it everywhere"..
"blowing with the wind of change"

The wind of change was blasting though the entire world. Soldiers took down their flags and saluted. Military bases were closed with tanks and jeeps leaving forever. The RAF base nearby to my hometown closed down, the British Soldiers and their Families moved away and the base was turned into a test site for high speed trains. It was a magic moment.

Finally and officially, WW II was over and we had new hope for the future. East and West were no enemies anymore, there was a brief moment when we thought that peace was possible.

Some month later, January 16th of 1991, Gorge W. Bush announced the start of "desert storm" to expel Iraqi forces from Kuwait. We just couldn't believe it.

They had told us for generations that war was such a terrible thing and that there were no winners in war. But here we were, back into war again. I remember a yellow "post it"-note placed on the bathroom mirror that morning of 1991 when I was getting ready for school.

It had been handwritten by my elder sister and said only a few words: *"We are at war"*. That couldn't be true. That morning everybody was discussing about how that was possible. We were in our teens and some in their early 20s and talked to our teachers about what was happening.

We saw live footage and patriot missiles on television 24/7. War was brought to us live in our living rooms by correspondents directly from Iraq. We were bombarded with videos showing live attacks. There were many protests on the streets against the war with the slogan *"no blood for oil"*.

Many elder GenXers were young soldiers in the Gulf War. The others were teenagers and couldn't believe what was happening. We had expected a war with the Soviet Union but not for oil.

To quote Kenan Thompson:

"I am Gen X, I just sit on the sidelines and watch the world burn".

24. SELF-REFLECTION

Most GenXers were raised to "pause and think". Figure out by ourselves what was right or wrong in all aspects of life. We knew, that if a plan had failed, *we* had committed a mistake and should try a different approach. The method of trial and error.

GenXers often blame *themselves* if something goes wrong, at work, in a relationship, in education. When we did something wrong as kids, it was *our* fault. We used to hear the phrase "why don't you use your brain?" all the time. Today if *our* kids do something wrong it must be their *parent's* fault. You can even hear the parents themselves saying: "well, if they behave like that it's only *my* fault". Wow. Wait a minute!? How did that happen? Why are *we* always the ones to blame?

You will never hear a Baby Boomer say, "yeah, that's *our* fault". The debt, the environment, the political situation, it's always someone *else's fault.* Mostly the younger generation's and the Millennials'. But also Millennials hardly take the blame, it's always somebody else's mistake. Mostly the Baby Boomers'. When we as Gen X did something wrong in our lives, *we* were the ones to blame and nobody else. Not the society, our parents or the school system. Everything was perfect but *we* were wrong. Today children have 'dyslexia' or 'ADHD'. We as kids were plain 'stupid', 'dumb' or 'boneheaded'. We have been called us "slackers" for all our lives, no matter what we have achieved.

Even now with us being in our forties and fifties we are constantly questioning ourselves and challenging ourselves to do better. We don't blame others automatically like many Baby Boomers and Millennials do. First we try to search the blame within ourselves. We know from the times we played alone as kids that if something *did* go wrong it actually *was* our fault.

The constant accusations by the previous generation made us sick, we did absolutely not want to be like that. Always blaming others for everything all the time. It's never their fault. Ever. We take our share of guilt for everything we've done wrong, but what about the other generations?

For many Millennials it is *never* their fault, if a relation doesn't work it's because the opposite sex is stupid, if they can't handle a task, it's because it's too hard and if there's anything wrong in their lives they blame others for it. That is mainly because they had been raised with the idea that they were perfect, with all their flaws, and society should accept them as they were.

I think that this has been the cause of depression for many, because the expectations were too high. They were often told *"you are perfect and society is ugly"*. Not only by their parents but by movies, songs (like "beautiful" by Christina Aguilera 2002), Ads and cartoons. Today there is a new approach to this topic, as the Australian author and speechwriter "Robert Hoge" explains: *"Don't tell the kids they are beautiful, tell them it's OK to look different"*. But for Millennials this wasn't the case. They were all told to be intelligent, beautiful and gifted. If something happened it was the teacher's fault, the other kids' or the system.

Also Baby Boomers have been raised in the center of attention. Their mother was always there, for them, cleaning and cooking and doing the household. Sacrificing her time and life for her kids only, no hobbies or spare time activities that took away the attention of the children. Many continued even long after their children were married, especially if the child was male. I know many Baby Boomers with their Silent Generation mom who still cares and cooks for them even if they are in their 60s and the mom in her 80's.

I guess that this is the main reason why Millennials and Baby Boomers fight so much all the time. Everybody blames the other, without listening or reflecting of any point the counterpart might be right. Nobody admits their mistakes, they are always the perfect ones and everybody else is wrong.

This makes us GenXers smile but it is actually a sad thing. Boomers and Millennials are demanding and aggressive generations, the negative energy is thrown in the face of the counterpart. Baby Boomers in the 1960s and 1970s organized riots, revolutions against their parents, against the system, loud, excessive and violent.

We were raised in a different way, more anti-authoritarian and independent. We were taught trough movies, songs and stories to respect the others and be kind. The problem is that our parents *told* us to be kind, self reflective and patient, but they themselves didn't behave that way either. We tried to be caring, understanding, helping others and show our weakness but that's not how real life works, especially when the others are loud, oppressive and self entitled.

We were raised to listen to the counterpart's opinion and points of view, but *our* side was *never* heard. Our teachers and parents, the Baby Boomers had a very rigid opinion and we were forced to follow their ideals. They were right and everybody else was wrong. No questions asked. They had fought for their new lifestyle and we were supposed to accept it for the only right idea.

Since they had forced their world view on us, we had decided (as every generation) to do the exact opposite of what our parents had done. We did not want to force others to have *our* opinion, never accept advice or doubt themselves. That's why Most GenXers don't care for hierarchy, we don't like to give orders or receive any. We work as single individuals in a team, no leaders needed.

Of course all young generations have rage against the system growing up, that wasn't any different for us. But unlike our parents we chose not to riot publicly and organize protests. That had been *their* thing, they had done that for ages. The 1968 and 1969 were famous for turmoil and yet again Woodstock.

So instead of throwing our anger out to the world, attacking the police and setting cars on fire, we adopted a different strategy. Our mini -protests were laughed at anyway, because their revolts had been so much more epic and revolutionary.

In the song "Killing in the Name" 1992 by the Gen X Band "Rage against the machine"lead singer Zack de la Rocha repeats one of the Gen X favorite slogans:

*"f**ck you , I won't do what you tell me!!!"..*

*"f**ck you , I won't do what you tell me!!!"..*

*"f**ck you , I won't do what you tell me!!!"..*

*"f**ck you , I won't do what you tell me!!!"..*

*"f**ck you , I won't do what you tell me!!!"..*

*"f**ck you , I won't do what you tell me!!!"..*

*"f**ck you , I won't do what you tell me!!!"..*

That was exactly our motto.

Whatever our parents had in mind for us, "go and find a job, pay off our debts, be part of the society we have planed for you, fill in the part we have prepared for you since you were born, start a family to give us grandchildren and pay our retirements, be exactly as we want you to be"

The answer was a sharp *no*!!

we *refused* to.

But we didn't *say* anything out loud. We simply *refused* ourselves to do it. No talking, no fights, not similar to anything that they had done to their parents. That would have been to easy, that's what they expected from us. Just passive, silent revolution. Being disobedient. Like the burning monk on the cover of the same CD by Rage against the machine in 1992.

Besides calling us slackers and cynical they often judged us to be disaffected. Which is a synonym for disobedient.

But they never understood that exactly *that* was our rebellion. They were better at fighting and arguing than us, they had trained all their lives with authority, their parents and police. They were ready to oppress any kind of revolution at the beginning, they had organized them before and knew how do dismantle them. But disobedience? What were they supposed to do against that? Yell and scream? Come on, we were used to that!

We are the masters of patience. Cynical, realists and thinkers. Result-orientated. We read people's intentions and recognize schemes. We wouldn't fall into the trap of doing exactly what they wanted us to do. *We just did not do it.*

It actually worked because it drove them crazy.

In the early 1990s with Kurt Cobain we had found the perfect representative. A young man with an ugly sweater singing self destructive songs. Not being flashy, sex-orientated, loud and oppressive. No "Woodstock"-like half naked screaming on the stage. In the 1970s most of the stars died very young by excessive abuse of toxic substances. Kurt Cobain died of what for our generation is the second cause of death for that age group:

Suicide. That alone speaks for itself.

Whereas the Baby Boomer generation threw their anger out into the world GenXers did the opposite. Our anger was projected against *ourselves*. We had heard so many times that we were "slackers" that we had a low self esteem and addressed that topic also music-wise. In the early 1990s with the grunge movement, many new bands came up that promoted self irony and even self hate.

Some songs talked about being a loser like "Loser" by Beck 1994:

"I'm a loser Baby, so why don't you kill me"

or having no self esteem as in "Self Esteem" by the Offspring 1994:

"I'm just a sucker with no self esteem".

They were also suicidal versions as in "settle for nothing" by Rage Against The Machine 1994:

"to escape the pain in an existence mundane read my writing on the wall - there's no one here to catch me when I fall - death is on my side.. suicide"

Also "Adam's Song" 1999 by Blink 182 was based on a real suicide of a 16 year old.

"I'm too depressed to go on- you'll be sorry when I'm gone"

Self-reflection, self-destruction, depression and suicide is a broad spread phenomenon especially among GenXers. Proximity to suicide and destructiveness behavior puts you at risk. Professionals call this "suicide contagion".

In 2004 "The Age" published an article by "Simon Castles" where he calls us *"The Suicide Generation".*

He had noticed that by 1990s the suicide rate rates in the US, Australia and New Zealand had tripled among young men aged 15 to 19. Female suicide rates are generally lower but there are believed to be actually more attempts.

In the years to come that trend shifted to the next age group. He sadly remarked that *"the same generation that were killing themselves as teenagers is the same generation that are killing themselves now"*. According to "Robert Putnam" in his book "Bowling Alone", those *"raised in the 1970s and 1980s were three to four times more likely to commit suicide"*.

In 2002, *2320* Australians took their lives, almost 50% of them were GenXers. There is never only one cause to a problem but several.

Our formative years, the problems we have been exposed to as a generation. Also the economic instability, the great change and uncertainty and the grand political dictum of Margaret Thatcher *"there is not such a thing as a society - only individuals"* caused anxiety.

In the Article *"Celebrity Suicide, all my heroes kill themselves and I'm sick to death of it"* published on July 23th 2017, the GenXer author Kylie Klein Nixon states that

"there is something deeply broken in my generation".

She lists some of the Gen-Xer Celebrities that have died of suicide or self endangerment throughout the years:

River Phoenix,

Kurt Cobain,

Michael Hutchence,

Elliott Smith,

Alexander McQueen,

Corey Haim,

Chris Farley,

Kristen Pfaff from Hole,

Dwayne Goettel from Skinny Puppy,

Jonathan Melvoin from the Smashing Pumpkins

Layne Staley and Mike Starr from Alice in Chains

Gidget Gein from Marilyn Manson

Paul Gray of Slipknot

Mikey Welsh from Weezer

Jason Molina

Scott Weiland

Chris Cornell from Soundgarden

and Chester Bennington of Linkin Park

This article was from 2017 so I sadly have to add

Dolores O'Riordan, lead singer of the cranberries, who died in 2018. She had written their best selling single "Zombie" in 1994 for taking distance from the IRA attacks that had killed two innocent children in Harrington (just like the Australian tourists in Roermond).

Our heroes, our peers. Our idols. All died horrible, desperate and lonely deaths. For the previous generations this is nonsense. The silent generation had survived a war, their life was essential to restart their countries, built houses and work on the economic growth.

Baby Boomers were all busy to expand, produce, work and achieve more. There was no space for depression in society and people with mental disorders were sent to lunatic asylums. That's why many elder generations don't understand depression. It's useless and stupid for them. They say "just go out and do something fun and it will go away.

Just be happy, don't be such a whiner." My personal favorite was *"I guess, you are too lucky, you have everything and now you are looking for something to cry about"*. But depression is a serious medical illness and doesn't "just go away".

With grunge music we finally had somebody to express our feelings. Nirvana, Pearl Jam and lots of other amazing bands let us embrace our darkness. Finally, we were not alone anymore but had found many other people that thought and felt the same way we did. Somebody who would express our feelings, anxieties, anger and fear, for a brief moment our *souls* had a *home*. We didn't need music to provoke us, cheer us up or make us dance. We wanted music to express our true feelings.

The band name itself "Nirvana" was perfect, a peaceful place where our troubled minds could find some relief. "Soul Asylum" was another great Gen X-band name, it is impossible that a name like that could be applied to a Baby Boomers' or Millennials' band. Just think about it.. aha, no!

One of the symbols for our Generation was a quiet young man in an ugly sweater, uncombed long hair and a guitar. No screaming, provoking Mike Jagger in skinny leather jeans or super sexy eccentric Freddie Mercury with colored costumes.

I will never forget the legendary "MTV unplugged"show with Kurt Cobain performing his epic songs with an acoustic guitar. I still have that CD of course! The Baby Boomers wouldn't understand what we even *liked* about that 'filthy guy'. They expected young performers to be provocative on stage, not shy and dressed in an old sweater. They were prepared for a kind of revolution that we've never given to them. That's why they are convinced that we've never had one. But we did. In a way that they didn't even notice until today. It was silent.

For a brief moment everything was perfect, we saw our favorite bands on stages, at festivals and couldn't wait for the next album to be released.

Sadly, on April 5th 1994 Kurt Cobain killed himself. We were paralyzed by the pain. he had been more than a songwriter, he had been a symbol of a generation. And we knew it. The mourning was real, the grief of a generation that had lost it's idol.

The Baby Boomers mocked us for *"listening to music of stupid people that killed themselves"* and the day of Kurt Cobain's death in the news they spoke mainly about famous Baby Boomers who had died the same day and had brought so much more important things to the world.

They had lost John Lennon to a killer, Bob Marley to cancer and Freddie Mercury to Aids, so our grief was completely ridiculed. Even in a moment of pain they downplayed our feelings, everything that *they* had was so much more important to the world and we should just forget about him..

"He even killed himself, what a loser! He didn't give a shit about you, his fans, like nobody ever does". It was much more than losing a singer. It became personal. We were shocked by the news. Even the GenXers who didn't even listen to his music, were upset by the mocking of the Baby Boomers in the weeks and years to come.

Many of us still listen to Pearl Jam, the Foo Fighters, the Smashing Pumpkins and other bands we liked when we were teenagers or in our early twenties.

That's what all generations do, they like the music from the times when they were young. It makes them go back to the good old days, when they were young and wild, without families to care about or jobs that eat up their soul. That's why every generation says that "their" music obviously is the best.

Let's not argue about that. "De gustibus non est disputandum", (Latin: there is no arguing about taste). This ancient Roman saying carries a very Gen X like - attitude: everybody has the right to like what they want.

We don't argue all the time that our music is *better* than everybody else's. Like the Baby Boomers do all the time. We listen to whatever we want to and you are free to do the same.

But leave our music alone, you have no idea what it means to us, you wouldn't understand. We are even happy if other generations don't like our music, it wasn't meant for them.

Live and let live.

25. LIFESTYLE

Many GenXers opposed themselves to the *traditional* way of settling down.

Many never got married or much later than our parents, most of us had their children in their late 30s and 40s. That's partially caused by economic problems but even the rich and famous had their kids later in life: Julia Roberts at 37 and 40, Jennifer Lopez at 38, Eva Mendez at 40, Nicole Kidman at 41 and so on. This didn't only make it a financial decision but other factors play a role, too.

Many of us never started a traditional family (boy and girl get married and have kids) but as you can notice on the "stick figure families" on people's cars, there are many new 'family' combinations:

People living on their own, with flatmates, two people and a pet, with their parents, friends, having children without being married, adopting children, single parents, kids from different partners, divorced people and so on. The combinations are endless and they are all OK. It took us a long time to be accepted. Not only same sex or mixed couples but also people living on their own or two people and a pet were discriminated against. Endless mockery at family parties or by society, on the street or by relatives. The Baby Boomers' generation fought for equal rights, but we were the first ones to actually try to live that way.

Our overall lifestyle changed completely from what the previous generations and the media had considered to be "the norm". Even our way of protesting was different. That's probably another reason why we are so overlooked. Our actions were much more subtle than the Baby Boomers'.

When you take a closer look, also the famous Gen X stars are much less self entitled and much more humble. Think of Jennifer Lopez (1969), Bradley Cooper (1975), Jason Bateman (1969) or Dwayne Johnson (1972). Even the characters they impersonate are more humble, with self irony and respectful.

Completely different from Joe Pesci, Al Pacino or Jack Nicholson. When you think of those characters they are always full of themselves. The goal is to destroy the opponent and convince him to change his mind. Even now in their seventies they can play a mean, aggressive and strong character and they can pull it off. When you think instead of Keanu Reeves (1964), Jason Sudeikis (1975) or Jason Momoa (1979), even if they are completely different in appearance, they all have the kind, humble, silent or reserved character. And it's not a matter of age at all.

Very few GenXers enjoy to be in the spotlight and can pull of a mean, selfish character. It just doesn't fit. That doesn't mean that we are weak – but the contrary.

Self reflection and taking in consideration the opponents' idea is not easy. It takes a lot of strength to show one's weakness, being respectful and open to dialogue. It is so much easier to have one fixed opinion, screaming it out to the world and forcing it on others. But that's not Gen X style. We are strong, modest, and self-critical. We don't attack, judge and humiliate the others. If we see no reason to stay we walk away.

That's the same thing we do in relationships. We try to live with friends, with our fiancè, have a family. Some are in a long distance relationship, some travel back and forth and many are obliged to change their home every now and then due to their job.

The job market asked us to be flexible and so our personal interests and lifestyle had to follow along.

It's still trial and error, we have to move to different places cities and continents. Some companies close, others fire us, and the next pays less salary with a lousier contract. The post Covid 19 situation will be even worse, I'm afraid.

We have to reinvent our lives all the time. New jobs, new home, new colleagues, sometimes new friends and a new partner.

We've *never* got a steady life. That creates a lot of background anxiety, stress and worries that the previous generation didn't have to go through.

We are warriors and fight every day for survival. But nobody even notices that. They think that we don't want to make sacrifices or are not able to find a good steady, highly paid job, like them in their days. Most Baby boomers have no idea what we are going through.

Most of our parents have known only one home and one job for all of their lives.

Lucky them.

26. THE GIVING GENERATION

As members of the MTV-generation we love music, playlists, top 10 songs and have always assembled our favorite mix tapes. Today we have changed devices but the basic idea is still the same: we keep "creating" our own playlist. We make one for the gym, for driving to work, chilling at home or even a special occasion. We have always taken the bands' albums and modified them.

Whereas Baby Boomers bought an LP and had to listen to it the way it was, we assembled our own compilation from scratch. It could be anything, a theme of a sitcom, a song from a sound-track, a classic piece, an unplugged version or something we had recorded from the radio

New generations take their phone, download Spotify or open YouTube and listen to playlists created by *others,* 'customized to your taste'.

We've always created our *own.* Even if it took us ages to make a mixtape. We bought a blank tape that was either 60 minutes total -30 minutes each side - or 90 minutes total with 45 minutes on side A and 45 on side B.

And that's how we assembled the whole thing: For the first song maybe we used a double tape-deck to copy one song from an existing tape to ours. That was easy.

For the next song we played our parents' LP's on full volume with the tape recorder right in front of the speaker and recorded the song with our little recorder, pushing play *and* record *temporarily.* Praying that nobody would ring the doorbell or use the hairdryer during these precious minutes.

The third song was the theme from our favorite sitcom. Easy you might guess. But there was no Netflix, Spotify, or Shazam, remember? So we actually had to *wait* for the sitcom to be on actual *television,* standing by the TV with the little recorder in our hands, pushing play and record the second the theme started.

The trickiest thing was recording songs from the radio. On TV we only had one shot, if we got it wrong maybe we had to wait for another week to get a second chance. But we knew the time and date the sitcom would be on. It was much harder on the radio. Sometimes we were standing by for hours before our favorite song came on. When the host announced our song, we would feel the adrenaline rush through our body, stand by the radio on full volume with the little recorder in our shaky hands and the biggest smile on our face.

We would try to get the cleanest cut possible, even if usually the beginning was cut off and in the end somebody would talk over it. But the happiness of having caught our favorite song on a *tape* was indescribable! Now we could listen to it whenever we wanted! Especially on our *Walkman,* a cassette-reading portable device created in 1978 by Sony. Piece by piece we created the desired album for that moment. It wasn't perfect and usually the last song was incomplete because it was impossible to calculate the time left on the blank tape.

Today this all sounds crazy, but without CDs and internet we had to be very creative and very, very patient. If we wanted to show our affection to somebody we would create a special gift: a "psycho tape". It was a tape with a "playlist" of all the songs we wanted to share with our friend or a special person in that moment. We all knew how much effort and time it took to create such a tape. So it was always a very appreciated gift.

After all, we are the *MTV-Generation*, we let the music speak for us. We communicate through sounds and images. Words in our world cannot describe a feeling like a melody or a picture can. We are also capable of capturing the intention of the creator of a mix tape and what he or she wanted to communicate to us. We don't need any words for that.

Mix-tapes were only the beginning. We started sharing with others by collecting music and giving it to friends. In the 1980s and 1990s if we wanted to listen to our favorite song we had to buy the whole album or wait for it to play on the radio. That's why if somebody recorded it for us that was the best gift ever! The gift wasn't the physical tape but the *emotions* you would *experience* listening to it.

We started sharing emotions. And we became experts at making playlists.

Yes, that was somehow against copyrights but we also bought lots of original CDs as soon as they had been invented and they were pretty expensive, too. Without the internet everything was pricy and difficult to obtain.

If we wanted to learn something, we had to hire a teacher and pay by the hour or buy the actual book and study by ourselves. Knowledge was expensive and rare. No Wikipedia, documentaries or films available 24/7, no free tutorials. If we were lucky we knew somebody in real life who could teach us something. For example a computer specialist who could show us how to fix a problem on our computer.

We had to make him come over (or go to his house), try to understand what he was talking about and pay full attention to him in that moment and take notes. Otherwise there was no way to recover the information without going back and make him explain again.

If we wanted to watch a new movie we had two options, the theaters or the famous video-rental franchising "Blockbuster" founded in 1985. New movies, first on VHS and later also on DVD, could be rented for a night.

The best films were always rented out for the first couple of weeks so we had to choose *another* movie instead. The prices were high and there was even a fine if we brought them back late (or if we didn't rewind the tape).

Some years later Blockbuster had also added video games to their offer but in 2013 all the local stores were closed. Since 2011 it is available online on Dish, for the nostalgic Blockbuster fans.

To watch any movie apart from TV we had to be very patient and pay lots of money for it.

Only after many, many years, on a Monday morning, February 14th - St Valentines' - in 2005, above a pizzeria and Japanese Restaurant in San Mateo, California, things would finally change forever:

Three GenXers, Chad Hurley, (1977) Steve Chen, (1978) and Jawed Karim (1979) activated the domain:

"www.youtube.com".

A user-generated platform where anyybody could upload, view, rate and share videos for free with everybody in the world. It was epic and changed the world forever.

Until that day we had to search and pay for literally *everything*. From that moment on we had people teaching things for *free,* by making tutorials, about anything one could imagine.

Farmers teach how to cut plants, plumbers how to fix a pipe, dancers show their moves and you can even learn how to play an instrument, all for *free*. All the knowledge of experts teaching about their special subject, how cool is that?

Nerds teach us how to fix our computer and grandmothers share their special recipes. And if we missed a detail we can go back and watch the video all over again. At any time, night or day. Without even knowing these people.

Today it seems the most natural thing in the world, but it isn't. These GenXers had decided to get away from the greedy thinking of the money driven Baby Boomers and going towards sharing knowledge and free services.

Free WiFi, free music, free videos, free teaching. A revolution. The revolution that Baby Boomers had always feared would come one day. GenXers have changed the world. Instead of *selling* everything they have decided to collect knowledge and *give if away for free.*

We don't have to pay for uploading or watching a tutorial. For the user it is completely free of charge.

For many Millennials now it's always "free, free for me, me, me!" but many don't realize it's *not* self understood. It's not for granted that many things are complimentary now.

It wasn't like this when *we* grew up and somebody wanted to change that. Somebody actually had decided to cut off with the old world of greed and make life easier for everybody. And those were the GenXers.

Free service for the customer and make the sponsors pay for the cost. We are a generous generation, without nobody even acknowledging it. The dawn of a new era. A new life of freedom, knowledge and sharing information. Changing the idea of possession and distribution once and for all. No more secrets. We share information, skills and ideas.

Many have payed a very high price for doing so. They got sued, persecuted, incarcerated. Like Julian *Paul Assange*, born in 1971. He is an editor, programmer and founder of Wikileaks. He shared with the world classified US Army and Government information in 2006 and now is incarcerated in England. He didn't surely do it for fame or money but for sharing information and long held secrets.

Also *Edward Snowden*, born in 1983, an ex CIA employee who copied and leaked classified information of NSA in 2013, revealing numerous global surveillance programs.

Information and knowledge for everybody. Available for free on the internet thanks to Google and YouTube. Another similar important invention was

Wikipedia:

On January 13th, 2001 Jimmy Wales (1966) and Larry Sanger (1968) registered the first free online Encyclopedia, where everybody could add content with no central control for the editing. In 2018 it has been the world's 5th most popular website. Yet again GenXers had created a free platform for sharing information. Also here everybody could add their personal knowledge and content. Most GenXers don't believe in hierarchy. We don't tell others what to do nor let anybody tell us what to do. We are quite confident that everybody has enough skills to add only content that would be relevant to the subject. Obviously that concept was completely misunderstood by people who instead of knowledge share opinions and emotions.

We accept everybody's ideas and opinions, maybe we'll reflect and then decide that they differ from our point of view, but on the contrary to the previous generations we don't use *censure* to silence ideas that are different from ours.

This has been a very silent yet powerful revolution. Taking knowledge from the privileged ones and giving it to everybody on the planet who has access to the internet.

Lately I have read an article where people call Gen Z the "YouTube Generation". That's total nonsense. **Generation X** is the YouTube Generation, we have *invented* it, that's our creation.

I loaded up my first video on YouTube in the summer of 2005, the year it all started. That's when most Gen Z were *born*. Only because we are not bragging about our ideas and inventions all the time doesn't mean that somebody else can take the credit for it.

Before YouTube and Wikipedia there had been other, more rudimentary websites, that we had used to search for, upload and distribute information.

In the 1980s and 1990s when we wanted to learn how to play a song on our guitar, we had to figure it out by ourselves. We played the song over and over again on our tape deck or CD player. The tape deck was actually better for this job because we could listen while rewinding or fast forwarding by pushing "Play" and "Rewind" or "Fastforward" contemporarily! Who doesn't remember this? What a terrible sound! We used to listen to the same piece over and over again until the tape got all caught up it the tape deck or it wore out. Then we tried to write down what we had captured.

This is how "misheard lyrics" were born, sometimes we were convinced to hear lyrics that in reality were completely different. Check out "misheard lyrics" videos on YouTube, they are hilarious!

So we could either spend our afternoons guessing lyrics and then pass them to our friends or search for expensive books of our favorite album and buy them.

If we were lucky to find them in a bookstore, otherwise they had to be ordered. Sometimes I bought one of the books and my friends would buy the other.

As many GenXers in the 1990s I played the guitar in a local rock band. We created our own songs and had some small gigs in local pubs. Sometimes we got together with other bands for a jam session and shared our guessed lyrics and chords to the latest songs and made our self "guitar books" which took ages to create. We taught each other the newest guitar riff or some tricks and spend lots of creative moments together. It was a slow process and always took a long time and guesswork.

Today on YouTube we have our favorite artists, Slash, Billy Corgan or John Frusciante explaining in person the guitar riffs to their songs. It's still amazing to me.

In 1992 a website under the domain "www.OLGA.net" collected tab sheets and lyrics by musicians who wanted to share them on forums. Finally we could share lyrics and chords without spending hours and hours trying to "guess" the right chords or lyrics, it was revolutionary. But as expected 1996 EMI Publishing had filed a complaint about breaching copyright law and OLGA was shut down. The site came back later for being sued and closed again in 2006 and in October 2019 the site has been taken offline.

Eugeny Naidenov has invented a similar site called "Ultimate Guitar.com" in 1998 in Kaliningrad where the songwriters receive a compensation for the display of the tabs. This is one of the last surviving Tab-Websites. Guitar Tabs and My Guitar Tabs have gone dark as well.

A similar thing happened to Napster, founded by Shawn Fenning (1980) and Sean Parker (1979) in 1999. Its technology allowed participants to share their MP3 files with others.

The heavy metal band Metallica sued Napster in the year 2000 for violation of copyright and the original service was shut down. The name survived after the assets were liquidated and purchased by other companies. Most similar websites have faced similar copyright claims over the years. But the music industry had to give in at some point.

In 2006 Daniel Ek (1983) and Martin Lorentzon (1969) created Spotify, a freemium service. The basic features are free with advertisement and the commercial-free version via paid subscription. This is a similar service as offered by YouTube, you can chose between the free version with ads or pay for the premium version without ads.

This is the next step, you can *choose* if you want to pay for the service or receive it for free, making the sponsors pay for their ads. Many GenXers have revolutionized the market, creating new, more affordable and accessible services for all. Rich and poor, all over the globe. Making our lives so much easier.

If you want an example of what GenXers really can achieve, take a look at *Elon Musk* (1971):

The engineer, industrial designer and CEO of Tesla and chief designer of Space X has declared that his goal is to

"change the world and help humanity, reduce global warming through sustainable energy".

In Tesla he just handed out an "anti handbook handbook" to his employees. The first line reads:

"We're Tesla, we're changing the world. We're willing to rethink everything".

That already says a lot about the approach towards his employees. He doesn't say "I am the boss, I decide and you do what I tell you to do".

He says we *are* Tesla. We, everybody. It's an unconventional handbook and that's the point. It doesn't *"tell you how poorly you can behave before you get shown the door"*. He is bringing all the GenXers qualities together:

Think outside the box.

Do unconventional things.

Change the world.

He wants everybody who has a great idea to solve a problem to e-mail or talk directly to their manager or to a VP or even to himself. No hierarchy to stop the success of the company. No rules just for the sake of the rules.

He even takes it one step further: he wants his employees to *behave* like GenXers:

Be reliable and on time without anyone checking on you.

Be creative.

Be exceptional.

Work for the company not for the CEO or for your manager.

Forget the old rules and make your own.

This is exactly what he does. And it shows amazing success.

There are more and more GenXers now as CEO s and start-ups are 51% by GenXers. The Baby Boomer bosses retire and often Millennials take their places. There is more publicity around them of course because they like the attention.

Gen Xers don't have a problem with hierarchy because they don't even care for titles. Even Elon Musk states:

" I consider myself more the lead engineer than the CEO of Tesla".

He has founded several companies, is CEO and CTO of Space X (X!), founder of the Boring Company and was ranked joint-first on the Forbes list of "The most innovative Leaders of 2019".

He shows all the GenXers characteristics and surprises each time with his unconventional creativity. Meanwhile Baby Boomers and Millennials are fighting about who is going to save the world. Maybe it will be the GenXers with their innovative ideas. Just saying.

Speaking of which, as I listed in the beginning most statistics give us only 15 years, from 1965 to 1980. But if we had the full 20 years as the other generations we would surely include the cuspers from 1963, like Whitney Houston, Michael Jordan and Quentin Tarantino. Also Jeff Bezos (1964), the Founder and CEO of Amazon. We would count Venus (1980) and Serena Williams (1981), Edward Snowden (1983), Marie Kondo (1983) and many others. All creative, innovative and unconventional people.

27. EPILOGUE

So here we are now, in our forties and early fifties, still trying to find out what life is all about. Despite all expectations we have become adults, but luckily without "growing up" in the conventional term. We are still creative and independent, flexible thinkers. We are tough and can adapt to anything. I saw that during Covid-19 lock-down. In Italy we couldn't leave our houses for 55 days in a row. Police was patrolling the streets and there was a heavy fine for transgressors.

I saw Baby Boomers and Millennials going crazy having to stay inside. For us it was like going back in time, all alone in our room for hours and hours, trying to do something new or listen to music. Boredom? We can deal with that. We transform it into creativity.

Absurdity? Our world has always been crazy. We don't go insane because we *expect* the worst to happen. It takes the surprise element out. We are the *cool* generation, remember? While others are still shocked we can focus and find the solution. GenXers just rock :)

We are not apathetic but calm and focused to elaborate a plan to take over the world. Meanwhile Jeff Bezos and Elon Musk are racing to colonize mars.

Elon is also trying to save *this* planet, but you know, just in case it might be to late, he is working on plan B. Always thinking ahead.

Yet again, be careful, other generations, don't mock us because you think we are *weak*. We are humble and kind, but persistent, indestructible and patient.

We are creative and unconventional, we can come up with ideas you don't even dream of.

Be prepared.

The best is yet to come.

THANKS TO

my mom for being the exception that proves the rule

my husband Davide for his support

my sisters Daniela and Sarah

The Arnold Family

The 'Royal Fishbones', 'Puke Your Guts'

and all their fans

Susanne, Melanie, Kerstin and Andrea

Wiebke, Sabine, Anja and Sibylle

Alinza Valinza and Chriarinza

The entire combriccola

Rosi, Hilla and Birgit

Elina for her inspiration

Enrico, Mattia, Rossella

Francesca Qian

and all the wonderful people in my life